Regulation and Reform of the Housing Finance System

Regulation and Reform of the Housing Finance System

Patric H. Hendershott
and
Kevin E. Villani

American Enterprise Institute for Public Policy Research
Washington, D.C.

Patric H. Hendershott is professor of economics and finance in the
Krannert Graduate School of Management at Purdue University.

Kevin E. Villani is acting director of the Division of Housing Finance
Analysis in the Department of Housing and Urban Development.

Library of Congress Cataloging in Publication Data

Hendershott, Patric H
    Regulation and reform of the housing finance system.

    (AEI studies ; 210)
    1.   Housing—United States—Finance.   I.   Villani,
Kevin E., joint author.   II.   Title.   III.   Series:
American Enterprise Institute for Public Policy Research.
AEI studies ; 210.
HD7293.H46   332.7'2   78-12235
ISBN 0-8447-3312-1

AEI Studies 210

Printed in the United States of America

CONTENTS

1
Introduction

The U.S. financial system is one of the most highly developed in the world. Savers have a wide variety of instruments, with varying degrees of risk, maturity, and marketability, from which to choose. Similarly, borrowers may issue numerous forms of debt to suit their needs. Many observers list the efficiency of the financial system as a significant factor contributing to the high growth and prosperity of the U.S. economy.

The current system is not the product of some grand design, but the result of a continuous evolution of financial institutions and markets, sometimes influenced by governmental actions. New types of thrift institutions developed and flourished in the 1800s in response to the demands of the marketplace. Mutual savings banks, for example, were originally known as "5¢ savings banks," a nickname reflecting their emphasis on small deposits. Their initial purpose was to encourage thrift among people of little means by providing a savings vehicle. Savings and loan associations, known in many areas as building and loans, were created to tap pools of small savings in order to finance capital-intensive housing construction.

The Great Depression crumbled the fragile base of the financial structure that market forces had built. The risk of loss to household depositors and the lack of sufficient liquidity for existing financial institutions were blamed for the failure of the system. Government institutions were established to provide this insurance and liquidity. Currently, the Federal Deposit Insurance Corporation (FDIC) and Federal Savings and Loan Insurance Corporation (FSLIC) provide the insurance to commercial bank and thrift depositors, respectively. Liquidity is provided for commercial banks by the Federal Reserve System and for thrifts by the Federal Home Loan Bank System.

The resulting system worked extremely well for several decades. Financial institutions rarely failed, and when they did it was due to poor management or fraud; even then, depositors seldom lost money. Interest rates moved within a fairly narrow range, and credit was allocated efficiently. Capital was plentiful for housing, business, and government investment. Depository institutions prospered. All of this occurred in the presence of a plethora of restrictions on portfolios of thrifts (largely home mortgages for assets and short-term deposits for liabilities), on types of home mortgages (only standard payment mortgages were permitted, variable and graduated payments were prohibited), on some lending rates (because of usury laws in many states and FHA/VA ceilings), and on yields on deposits at commercial banks (Regulation Q, which limited the rate commercial banks could pay on savings deposits and forbade interest on demand deposits, has existed since 1936).

Because of the low level and general stability of interest rates, these restrictions brought only minor problems. In effect, the restrictions did not act as effective constraints on the behavior of profit-maximizing institutions. Since 1965, however, interest rates have risen substantially and have exhibited great volatility. The restrictions have become effective and have caused a number of problems and inequities. Small savers have been cheated out of a fair return, some households have been rationed out of the home mortgage market and thereby prevented from purchasing a home, and thrifts have been threatened with insolvency. A deluge of proposals to reform the system—largely to remove the restrictions—has resulted.

The Existing Housing Finance System

The term *financial system* refers to the mechanism by which funds flow from savers to ultimate borrowers. This mechanism encompasses the various private and public financial institutions, the financial instruments or securities and the laws, regulations, and customs governing the activities of the institutions and the terms under which the securities may be issued and purchased. Economists often discuss a hypothetical model of a "perfect capital market" in which such laws, regulations, and customs have little or no influence on the distribution of funds. The current U.S. financial system is a distant cousin to this hypothetical model. The structure of the housing finance system, in particular, contains numerous forms of regulation and intervention designed to alter the ultimate distribution of funds in favor of investment in housing. It follows that changes in this financial structure could have a significant impact on the distribution of savings among competing borrowers and thus on alternative forms of nonfinancial capital investment.

Savers are at the heart of the financial system; they provide their surplus funds to other units by purchasing their liability issues. Most of these surplus funds are provided by households. A much smaller share derives from businesses, which generally reinvest their savings rather than making them available to other units. Governments also "save" and invest in financial instruments or retire debt when they run surpluses (when tax receipts exceed expenditures).

A diagram of the U.S. financial system is presented in Figure 1. The diagram shows, via solid lines, the flow of funds from surplus units to household mortgage borrowers to other borrowers and to

FIGURE 1

The Flow of Savings and Interest Earnings

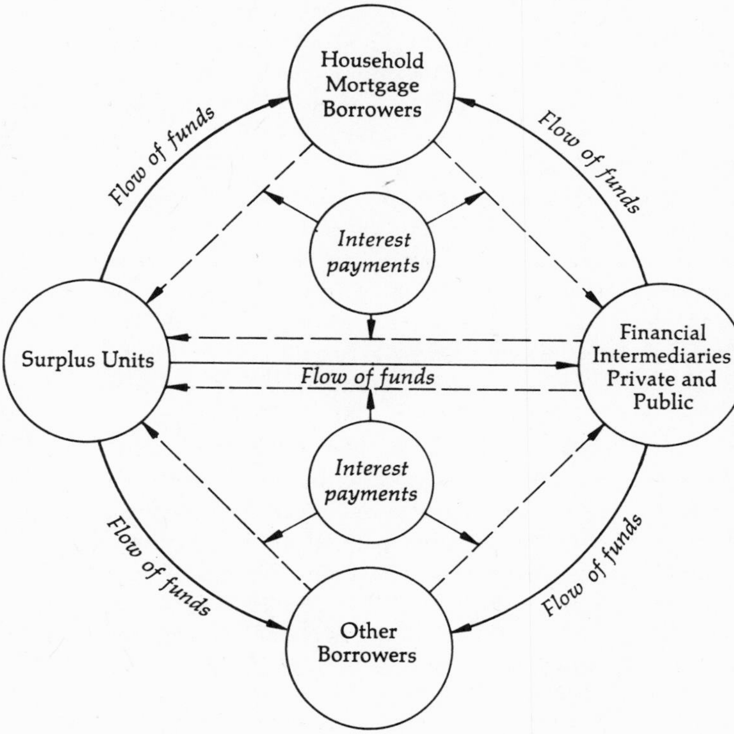

financial intermediaries, who then channel the funds to ultimate borrowers. Mortgage borrowers are singled out in order to highlight the implications of the financial structure for the flow of funds to this market, that is, to emphasize the housing finance system. The diagram also indicates, by dashed lines, the reverse flow of interest payments from borrowers to lenders.

As illustrated in the figure, surplus units may invest in mortgages, in nonmortgage primary securities, and/or in the liabilities of financial intermediaries. The first issue to be considered is, what determines the allocation of funds among these alternatives? The answer is, in significant measure, the particular characteristics of the financial instruments issued by ultimate borrowers and intermediaries and the needs of the surplus units. A mortgage, for example, is extremely cumbersome and administratively difficult for an individual household to manage. This explains why direct household investment in mortgages is quite minor. In fact, the arrow in the upper left, running from ultimate savers to household mortgage borrowers, could be removed without doing violence to reality. The choice of surplus units, then, is really between nonmortgage primary securities (corporate bonds and open-market paper, state and local government obligations, and Treasury bills, notes, and bonds) and intermediary claims which institutions tailor to meet the diverse needs of surplus units. Commercial banks, for example, offer transactions account services (demand deposits); and banks and thrifts—savings and loan associations, mutual savings banks, and credit unions—offer virtually riskless, interest-earning liquid deposits. Life insurance companies offer a package of pure (term) life insurance and savings (cash value), the interest return on which is tax-exempt. Private pension funds and state and local government retirement funds provide a vehicle for the accumulation of retirement savings, again with tax exemption during the period of accumulation, to finance annuities and pension benefits. Similarly, the liabilities of other financial intermediaries have characteristics tailored to some particular need of surplus units. These needs and the responses of intermediaries to them are a major determinant of the total flow of funds to private intermediaries.

In addition to the private financial intermediaries, such as those mentioned above, there are numerous federally sponsored credit agencies operating in the financial markets. The most prominent of these are Fannie Mae (the Federal National Mortgage Association), Ginnie Mae (the Government National Mortgage Association), and Freddie Mac (the Federal Home Loan Mortgage Corporation). These institutions generally issue credit market instruments in a variety of short and intermediate maturities, usually in fairly large ($25,000) minimum denominations. The funds raised are then re-lent to a particular class of borrowers, in most cases to homebuyers.

Finally, surplus units may invest directly in the issues of nonmortgage borrowers. This type of investment for the most part requires both larger denominations of funds and a greater degree of sophistication than does investment in the liabilities of the private intermediaries. Nonmortgage primary securities have a variety of risk, maturity, and marketability characteristics and, in addition, enjoy several tax advantages. Capital gains income on corporate equities is currently taxed at one-half the normal federal rate, for example, and the income from most issues of state and municipal governments is exempt from federal tax. Similarly, some types of Treasury securities receive favorable estate tax treatment.

We have thus far discussed some of the determinants of the distribution of surplus funds between nonmortgage primary securities and claims of financial intermediaries. A second issue, and an important one given that most funds are channeled through financial intermediaries, is what determines the choice between mortgage and nonmortgage assets by financial intermediaries. Again, this choice is significantly influenced by laws, customs, and regulations. Commercial banks emphasize commercial and industrial loans, for example, largely by custom. Mutual savings banks and particularly savings and loan associations invest heavily in standard fixed-payment mortgages as a result of substantial federal tax incentives, regulations (the institutions are limited in the types of nonmortgage securities they may hold), and custom (many are still called building and loan associations). Most federally sponsored credit intermediaries are limited by their charters to investment in single forms of assets, usually residential mortgages.

While laws, regulations, and customs, which together make up the financial structure, influence and in some cases determine the investment choices of individual surplus units and financial institutions, this structure is far from the entire story. Just as workers prefer high wages to low, and apartment owners high rents to low, lenders (households as well as institutions) prefer high interest income to low. Households with significant financial wealth will shop around among different types of intermediary claims and primary securities to obtain the best risk-adjusted after-tax expected return. Even households with quite limited wealth will compare yields on low-denomination intermediary claims. And financial institutions will, where permitted, compare yields on the entire spectrum of primary securities.

The aggregate distribution of funds is determined by supply and demand in the individual credit markets. Interest rates in these markets move to balance the supply of funds provided to these markets with the demands of borrowers. If, for example, the demand for funds by nonmortgage borrowers exceeds the total funds supplied directly and through intermediaries, then interest rates will rise in this market. In response, surplus units will divert some investment from intermediary claims (deposits) directly to the nonmortgage borrowers. In addition, some financial institutions will switch from other lower-yielding assets to the now higher-yielding nonmortgage asset. Finally, the higher yield itself will reduce the demands of borrowers in this market. The financial system achieves "equilibrium" when all interest rates and payment flows have adjusted such that borrowers have all the funds they demand at the rates charged in their market.

Government actions have influenced the allocation of funds by creating institutions that invest heavily in mortgages and by attempting to induce surplus units to allocate a large share of their funds to these institutions. The most prominent actions to create mortgage-specializing institutions are the inducements given to the growth of the federally sponsored credit agencies and the restrictions against investments, particularly of savings and loan associations, in non-mortgage securities. Investment in the liability issues of these institutions is encouraged by effectively guaranteeing the return on them, and by restricting the yields competitors (commercial banks) may pay on alternative instruments via deposit rate ceilings. The ultimate purpose of such actions is to bias the real capital stock in the economy in favor of housing. In terms of Figure 1, funds are shifted from nonmortgage primary securities to intermediary claims, and, because mortgage-biased institutions receive a greater share of intermediary receipts, the allocation of intermediary investment is shifted from nonmortgage primary securities to mortgages.

While the government actions have undoubtedly succeeded in increasing flows to the mortgage market and in lowering mortgage borrowing costs, the impact can be, and often is, overstated. A fallacy particularly common among policy makers is that direct measures to increase the supply of mortgage credit, such as mortgage investment by sponsored credit agencies, represent net additions to the aggregate supply of mortgage credit. This misconception stems from a failure to take into account interest rate adjustments and the accompanying portfolio responses of other investors. Because the increased supply of credit lowers yields, some private lenders are induced to leave the market. Moreover, low mortgage rates require low deposit rates at thrifts. If there are low interest payments flowing to thrifts (see Figure

1), then the interest payments flowing from thrifts must also be low, and this limits their ability to attract funds. Moreover, the costs of these actions—exaggerated housing cycles, due to sharp swings in periods of intermediation and disintermediation, and low deposit rates for savers—have often been underestimated.

History of Financial Reform Study Commissions and Legislative Proposals

The first major study of financial reform in the postwar era in the United States was undertaken in 1958 by the Commission on Money and Credit (CMC), a private group established by the Committee for Economic Development.[1] The CMC Report suggested a liberalization of the regulations that governed different intermediaries. In particular, the report called for allowing greater portfolio flexibility for thrift institutions. The report recognized the rate of portfolio restrictions in allocating credit to housing but argued that direct subsidies are a more efficient way of allocating resources than are regulations on the portfolio powers of financial institutions.

The CMC Report was the most comprehensive overview of the financial system produced up to that time. However, the total reform package was never seriously considered for implementation (although several individual recommendations were eventually enacted). The major reason was that the financial system, especially housing finance, was not perceived to be in any great difficulty at the time the report appeared. Thus the recommendations of the commission never got the political support they needed to become law.

By 1966, strains in the financial system appeared. High short-term interest rates and increases in rates on deposits offered by commercial banks generated a drain of funds out of thrift institutions and a sudden drop in housing activity. As a result, deposit rate ceilings at commercial banks were lowered; ceilings were extended to thrift institutions, with the thrifts allowed to offer a higher rate than commercial banks; and Congress authorized a study of savings and loan associations (SLAs). This study examined the role of the SLA industry and the Federal Home Loan Bank (FHLB) system in the economy and made numerous recommendations for reform.[2] Like its predecessor, it called for liberalization of the asset and liability restrictions on thrifts. It also recommended significant changes in the

[1] Report of the Commission on Money and Credit, *Money and Credit: Their Influence on Jobs, Prices, and Growth* (Englewood Cliffs, N.J.: Prentice-Hall, Inc., 1961).

[2] Irwin Friend, ed., *A Study of the Savings and Loan Industry* (Washington, D.C.: Federal Home Loan Bank Board, 1969).

FHLB advances mechanism through which FHLBS made loans to SLAS. First, advances (loans) would be available on request so that thrifts would have a guaranteed source of liquidity. Second, long-term advances would be made available to finance mortgages in capital-short areas, regardless of the state of the housing industry nationwide. The advances were to be financed by long-term FHLB security issues. These changes have been implemented in the 1970s. With respect to mortgage rate ceilings, the study recommended that state usury ceilings be set above the future anticipated competitive level and that Federal Housing Administration (FHA) and Veterans Administration (VA) ceilings be adjusted to levels such that the lowest yielding new mortgages would sell at par in the secondary market. Regrettably, these recommendations have not been adopted.

Again in 1969 interest rates rose sharply. Because of the 1966 change in interest rate ceilings, thrifts did not lose funds to commercial banks, but both they and banks lost funds (experienced disintermediation) to open-market instruments. Again, a large decline in housing activity occurred, and a panel was appointed to examine the flexibility and soundness of the financial structure. The panel, the presidential Commission on Financial Structure and Regulation, was charged with the duty of assuring that the nation's financial system would be able to respond to shifting needs while maintaining economic soundness.

The report of the commission, commonly called the Hunt Commission Report, recommended many of the same proposals advanced ten years earlier by the Commission on Money and Credit.[3] The Hunt Commission also contained a consistent plan for the gradual reduction of the regulatory restrictions placed on financial intermediaries, including the removal of interest rate ceilings on deposits, the relaxing of restrictions on thrift investment powers (including variable-rate mortgages, the interest rate on which varies with an index rate rather than being fixed for the life of the mortgage), and the extension of demand deposit authority to thrifts. Under this proposal relief could be provided through a system of direct subsidies, should there be problems in transition to this less restrictive financial system or should any sector or industry be particularly disadvantaged by the removal of the existing regulatory structure. Accordingly, the commission included in its report suggestions that would buttress the housing and thrift industries against any unforeseen problems during the transition period. Chief among these was a temporary tax credit for lenders who invested in home mortgages.

---

[3] U.S. President's Commission on Financial Structure and Regulation, *Report*, Washington, D.C., 1972.

The 1969 episode of disintermediation and housing decline prompted the Federal Reserve Board to undertake a study to examine possible ways of moderating short-term swings in the availability of housing credit.[4] The study recommended a major lengthening of the liabilities of thrifts, but only minor changes in the asset structure. The study also proposed the gradual removal of rate ceilings on mortgages and deposits. The ceilings were to be lifted only as other reforms that would provide for a healthy and competitive thrift industry were implemented. Variable-rate mortgages were not endorsed by the study because of the transfer of interest rate risk to household borrowers. Another proposal, which has since received little attention, was aimed at smoothing the flow of mortgage credit by stabilizing business investment. The study concluded that a variable business-investment tax credit would stabilize expenditures for residential construction as well as for plant and equipment.

The most recent study of the housing finance system is the Financial Institutions and the Nation's Economy (FINE) document circulated for comment by the House Subcommittee on Housing.[5] Unlike past studies that were motivated by the inflexibility of the existing system, this one appears to have been motivated by fear that the financial reform package being debated in the Senate would diminish the supply of mortgage credit. In order to assure that the housing sector would not suffer in a less regulated financial environment, the FINE document recommended government-sponsored interest rate risk insurance for mortgage lenders. In a similar vein, it recommended an expansion of the FHLB advances mechanism to finance long-term mortgage investment.

Some of the recommendations of the study commissions were developed into serious legislative proposals. The first is the Financial Services Center (FSC) proposal of the FHLB system. Its provisions follow closely the recommendations of the FHLB study in 1969. They are intended to transform savings and loan associations into family financial centers, providing a complete array of personalized financial services to households. The provisions of the FHLB proposal are perhaps best summarized by quoting from the FHLB publication:

> The Board is proposing that a wide range of family aids be
> provided by thrift institutions. These include the provision
> of checking account powers and other third-party payment

---

[4] *Ways to Moderate Fluctuations in Housing Construction*, Federal Reserve Staff Study, 1972.
[5] U.S. Congress, House of Representatives, Subcommittee on Financial Institutions Supervision, Regulation, and Insurance of the Committee on Banking, Currency, and Housing, *Hearings on Financial Institutions and the Nation's Economy "Discussion Principles,"* 94th Congress, 1st session, December 1975.

services, the ability to make consumer loans, the ability to offer financial counseling and planning, investment programs, and tax and trust services, all geared to the needs of the average family, and possibly other types of family finance services. In addition, since the family finance center package cannot, by itself, deal completely with the maturity imbalance between assets and liabilities of savings and loan associations [S&L's], we also believe, as we have indicated, that there is a strong need for S&L's to offer variable rate mortgages, along with fixed-rate mortgages, and to have a further means by which they can raise long-term money— in particular, through mortgage-backed bonds.[6]

The first attempt, in recent years, to legislate financial reform began when the Treasury Department released its embodiment of the Hunt proposals as the proposed Financial Institutions Act (FIA) of 1973.[7] The act moved towards the homogenization of thrift and commercial bank investment and liability powers. Thus, while still specializing in mortgage loans, thrifts would be given unlimited authority in the consumer credit area and limited options to invest in corporate debt; they could also offer demand deposit accounts. Deposit rate ceilings would be removed over time; interest rate ceilings on FHA and VA mortgages would be eliminated; and mortgage lending would be encouraged through the use of a tax credit of up to 3½ percent of the income received by a lender from residential mortgages.

As FIA moved through the Senate, the housing aspects of the bill began to take on more and more importance, and some modifications were made to favor the mortgage market. These modifications became more pronounced when this legislation was considered in the House. At this point it is interesting to note the evolution of the movement toward financial reform. The first postwar study offered suggestions to increase the flexibility and viability of the financial system.[8] Little attention was directed toward "protecting" the housing market from the forces of competition. It was believed that housing goals could be more effectively achieved outside the financial system, and that housing, like all other sectors of the economy, would benefit from a more efficient and equitable financial structure. By the time financial reform was considered by the House in 1976, attention

---

[6] Federal Home Loan Bank Board, *A Financial Institution for the Future*, Washington, D.C., 1975, p. 625.

[7] U.S. Congress, Senate, Subcommittee on Financial Institutions of the Committee on Banking, Housing, and Urban Affairs, *Hearings on the Financial Institutions Act of 1973*, 93rd Congress, 1st session, November 1973.

[8] Report of the Commission on Money and Credit, *Money and Credit*.

had shifted to the need for a strong and secure housing sector. The housing downturn in 1973–1974, which, in many respects, was symptomatic of the inflexibility of the financial system, became the focal point of the legislation.

The House version of financial reform reflected the recommendations of the FINE document, which, in part, was intended as the antithesis of the FIA.[9] Hearings were held in December 1975 on the FINE document, and the full committee heard testimony the following March on the resulting Financial Reform Act (FRA) of 1976.[10] The approach taken by most of the expert witnesses testifying on this bill was to contrast the provisions of the FRA with the provisions of the FIA in the Senate, usually to the detriment of the former. Several of the FRA provisions broke with the recommendations of the FINE study. The proposed gradual elimination of deposit rate ceilings, for example, was replaced by a recommendation that a Deposit Interest Rate Control Committee set rate levels and rate differentials between commercial banks and thrifts so as to protect housing.

A major proposal in the Financial Reform Act of 1976 to alter the current FHLB advances system also illustrates the increasing bias of proposed legislation in favor of housing. Specifically, the Federal Home Loan Bank Board (FHLBB) would be empowered to grant long-term advances (up to thirty years) to all financial intermediaries during periods of pressure on mortgage markets. These advances would be granted for the purpose of providing mortgage loans at below-market rates. Thus, advances, which were originally designed as a liquidity backup to enable SLAs to finance housing when deposit inflows slowed, were now being advocated as a permanent source of funds to supplement private deposits.

Overview of Study

Although the existing financial structure worked well during the 1950s and early 1960s, it obviously was not sufficiently flexible to adjust to the sharp rise in interest rates between late 1965 and early 1970. Portfolio restrictions requiring maturity imbalance by thrifts

---

[9] U.S. Congress, House of Representatives, Subcommittee on Financial Institutions Supervision, Regulation, and Insurance of the Committee on Banking, Currency, and Housing, *Hearings on Financial Institutions and the Nation's Economy, "Discussion Principles,"* 93rd Congress, 1st session, November 1973.

[10] U.S. Congress, House of Representatives, Subcommittee on Financial Institutions Supervision, Regulation, and Insurance of the Committee on Banking, Currency, and Housing, *Hearings on the Financial Reform Act of 1976,* 94th Congress, 2nd session, March 1976.

11

threatened the viability of that industry and thus of housing finance. In addition, the inflexibility of the standard fixed-payment mortgage instrument limited the ability of some households to make their first home purchase.

The most obvious solution would have been the encouragement of homeownership through innovations in the mortgage instrument and of maturity balance by thrifts. While numerous steps in these directions have been taken during the 1970s, the response in the second half of the 1960s was largely one of increased market regulation and intervention. Usury laws, FHA/VA rate ceilings, and a vastly expanded role in the home mortgage market by the federally sponsored credit agencies were all employed in an attempt to mitigate the rise in the home mortgage rate and the threatened decline in homeownership and housing production. Rather than removing restrictions on the portfolios of thrifts to enable them to compete for deposits on an equal footing with commercial banks, deposit rate ceilings were enforced to limit the ability of banks to compete. The primary benefit of the present highly regulated system (relative to one without deposit rate ceilings, restrictions on thrift portfolios, or intervention in the home mortgage market by the sponsored credit agencies) has been to mortgagors, that is, homeowners. The primary costs have been low interest for depositors, sharper cycles in homebuilding, and the resultant greater housing costs and prices.

Removing deposit rate ceilings—and the consequent inequities for depositors and cycles for housing—is the dominant thrust of financial reform. Thus, the vast majority of reform proposals include the removal of the ceilings and the establishment of compensating provisions to maintain the viability of thrifts. Proposals deal with the viability of thrifts over both the short-run (the cycle) and the long-run. Consideration of alternative roles politicians would like the financial structure to play and of political obstacles to previous reform is a necessary component in the development of a workable reform package.

2

Inflation, Rising Interest Rates, and Problems for Thrifts and Homeowners

In spite of a plethora of regulations, the financial system put in place during the Depression performed admirably prior to 1966 because interest rates were relatively stable. The annual average Moody's AAA seasoned corporate bond rate stayed within the 2½ percent to 4½ percent range throughout the entire 1939–1965 period. Moreover, fluctuations in the rate were relatively minor, with most of the changes within this range reflecting a gradual increase during the 1950s. Similar stability is observed for intermediate term rates; the average annual yield on three- to five-year U.S. government bonds varied between just under 3 percent and 4½ percent during the 1955–1965 period. In the second half of the 1960s, rates rose sharply and have since oscillated around a much higher level. Between 1969 and 1976 the same Moody's bond rate varied between 7 percent and 9 percent, and the three- to five-year U.S. rate has been within the 5.75 percent to 8 percent interval.

The principal cause of the increase in interest rates between 1965 and 1969 was a far too expansionary fiscal policy. The attempt by the federal government to wage a war in Vietnam without significantly raising taxes or reducing nondefense outlays—the full-employment budget surplus declined almost monotonically from plus $5 billion in late 1964 and early 1965 to minus $15 billion in the middle of 1968—created a substantial excess demand for funds and thus raised interest rates. Interest rates remained high during the 1970s for a number of reasons. Occasional overly expansive monetary policies (particularly in 1972), the world food and raw material shortages, and the actions of the oil cartel produced even higher observed, and then expected, inflation rates. These have generated inventory and fixed-capital investment demands, the financing of which kept interest rates high. The

13

slowdown in inflation accompanying the most recent recession and recovery has moderated this tendency somewhat, but the financing of massive federal deficits ($71 billion in 1975, $58 billion in 1976, and $51 billion in 1977) has prevented more than a normal cyclical decline in interest rates. This rise in the general level of interest rates created problems for the thrift industry, homebuyers, and the housing industry.

Problems Created for Thrift Institutions

There are three types of financial intermediaries, in addition to commercial banks, that accept household deposits: (1) savings and loan associations, (2) mutual savings banks, and (3) credit unions. All share several characteristics. First, they finance their asset purchases for the most part by issuing savings "shares," or deposits, that are approximately equivalent to savings accounts at commercial banks. Second, virtually all their deposits are owned by households. Third, most savings and loan associations and all mutual savings banks and credit unions have mutual charters; that is, they are "owned" by the depositors, not stockholders.

The primary investment of thrift institutions is residential (predominately single family) mortgages. Savings and loan institutions, by custom, law, and regulations, are limited almost exclusively to mortgage investments. Mutual savings banks have somewhat more flexibility, but still invest proportionately large amounts in home mortgages. In terms of total deposits, savings and loan associations are about three times as large as mutual savings banks and nine times as large as credit unions. The thrift industry is thus often described as consisting of firms engaged in intermediation between the household deposit and home mortgage market.

The deposit maturities of thrift institutions are effectively limited to six years or less (eight years as of June 1978) by deposit rate ceilings.[1] Correspondingly, thrifts are largely prohibited from investing in many short-term assets or assets whose yield adjusts rapidly to changes in the general level of interest rates: business loans, consumer credit, and variable-rate mortgages. The result is the asset-liability imbalance of thrift portfolios, the major source of the problems of the housing finance system.

The following discussion considers the problems of engaging in

---

[1] See chapter 7 for an explanation of this point.

14

maturity intermediation in a volatile financial environment.[2] Implicitly, these are the problems thrifts would have faced beginning in 1966 had deposit rate ceilings not been imposed. For the purpose of our discussion we shall assume that thrifts function in competitive markets but with the existing portfolio restrictions requiring portfolio imbalance. That is, both short-term deposit rates, which are assumed to be related to short-term open-market rates, and home mortgage rates are determined by competitive market forces and are given to thrifts.

In theory, maturity intermediation—the borrowing of short-term funds to finance purchases of long-term mortgages—is profitable if the effective cost of short-term borrowing is less than the effective yield on mortgages over the life of the mortgage loan. The expected effective cost of funds can be calculated by forecasting short-term rates, and it can then be compared with current mortgage rates and a forecast of default losses. If the forecasts are accurate, and the spread between the effective mortgage and deposit rates is sufficient, then the loan will be profitable. In practice, difficulties arise even if thrifts are accurate forecasters. The first is potential negative cash flows. Given that short-term interest rates vary cyclically, maturity intermediators will experience negative cash flows when short-term rates are high and positive cash flows when rates are low. Viewed from a balance sheet perspective, the same forces that generate cycles in short-term interest rates will produce cycles in yields on mortgages. These cycles will induce inverse fluctuations in the market value of the long-term mortgage portfolio and net worth of thrifts. This may result in a second problem: if the rise in rates is of sufficient magnitude, net worth becomes negative—the firm is technically insolvent.

The problem of temporary negative cash flows can be solved by temporarily increasing borrowing, that is, borrowing to pay the interest on existing debt. Negative net worth could present more of a problem because private lenders, such as commercial banks, would probably be unwilling to lend to technically insolvent firms, and bankruptcy could result. A guaranteed source of liquidity would thus appear to be a prerequisite for a firm to engage in substantial maturity intermediation.

Another problem could arise even for firms with perfect foresight regarding future deposit costs. If long-term rates are currently low and expectations of higher future short-term rates develop, then

---

[2] See George Kaufman, "A Proposal for Eliminating Interest-Rate Ceilings on Thrift Institutions, A Comment," *Journal of Money, Credit, and Banking*, August 1972, pp. 735–43, for a similar discussion.

unregulated investors would switch from long-term securities into short-terms until the long-term rate equalled the average of expected future short-term rates plus a liquidity premium. If the mortgage rate appeared to be too low relative to these expectations, thrifts would purchase an equally risky short-term asset such as a business loan. Competitive market forces would, in this manner, drive the mortgage rate up to be consistent with these expectations. But mortgage lending thrift institutions are denied this option. They must either make mortgage loans, invest in riskless Treasury securities that often yield less than their deposits cost, or cease operations. Because mortgage rates are determined by supply and demand in this market, an individual firm that anticipates a trend of rising interest rates does not have the ability to raise its rate. Even if the entire industry forecasts higher future deposit costs, they may not be incorporated in current mortgage rates because firms are effectively prohibited from driving them up by withholding funds from the mortgage market. If the anticipated rise in deposit costs occurred, insolvency of thrifts would be a real possibility.

Beyond this is the problem of forecasting short-term interest rates accurately for up to twenty-five or thirty years into the future. This would seem to require forecasting unusual or earthshaking occurrences like great depressions, major wars, and long-term energy or raw materials shortages, as well as more mundane events such as oil embargoes, inventory cycles, swings in monetary policy, and national elections. Near-term events are important because of the importance of the precise pattern of future rates, not just the effective long-run cost of borrowing. The principal on a mortgage is amortized over the life of the mortgage, implying that near-term future rates are more important than distant-term rates. In fact, given that mortgage issues are callable by the household issuer, more distant future short-term rates themselves become a factor in calculating the average cost of future deposits invested in the mortgage. No financial market analyst can forecast future interest rates with enough confidence to warrant the degree of maturity intermediation implied by the current asset and liability structure of most thrifts. Thus improved forecasting is not a practical solution to the problem of maturity imbalance.

The rise in interest rates since 1965 clearly illustrates the threat of unforeseen rate increases to the viability of the savings and loan industry. The upward trend in rates followed a long period of stability and was not anticipated by either thrifts or other participants in the financial markets. Few foresaw the massive buildup in Vietnam, and even fewer anticipated the refusal to finance the war by higher taxes or limitations on the expansion of other federal programs. In an environment where interest rates, including those on deposits, are determined competitively, an unexpected rise in interest rates of this magnitude would have caused the vast majority of the savings and loans to fail. In the absence of Regulation Q, commercial banks, which do not have a maturity imbalance between their deposit liabilities and assets, would have paid deposit rates in line with the higher short-term open-market rates. Thrifts would have either paid these higher rates or lost their deposits; in either case bankruptcy would have been the end result.

The significant possibility of this outcome makes it difficult to imagine thrifts voluntarily engaging in substantial maturity intermediation in the absence of federal insurance of deposits. Households would probably require such large risk premiums (high deposit rates) that such intermediation would not be profitable. The existence of deposit insurance (and limited stockholder liability for nonmutual institutions) changes the situation. Losses for incorrect decisions would be borne in large measure by the insurer (taxpayers), while the additional returns for correct decisions would accrue to the depositors (and shareholders). This asymmetry suggests that thrifts would pursue a high-risk (maturity imbalance) investment strategy at the ultimate expense of taxpayers, even if deposit rate ceilings and investment restrictions were removed. In the presence of deposit insurance a case can be made that thrifts should be required to balance their portfolios, rather than be prohibited from balancing them.

Problems for Homeownership

It has often been argued that inflation has a particularly severe impact on the demand for homeownership. This impact is said to result from the monthly payment and the downpayment required to finance the purchase of a home with a standard fixed-payment mortgage instrument.

The problem with respect to monthly payment levels results from the rise in nominal mortgage rates during inflationary periods. Past inflation generally gives rise to anticipation of future inflation. In an unrestricted financial system without taxes, savers and borrowers switch between securities until nominal interest rates rise by the amount of the anticipated inflation, restoring real rates of interest to their pre-inflation level. Suppose, for example, that the real rate of interest is 3 percent, and anticipated inflation increases from zero to 3 percent. The rise in the nominal mortgage rate from 3 to 6 percent will approximately double the current monthly mortgage payment. The real payment burden will also be doubled, because the price level has not yet moved. Subsequent real monthly payments will fall throughout the life of the mortgage, assuming the expected inflation is realized.

This "tilting" of real monthly payments has created cash-flow problems for households during the past decade, as can be seen by comparing the change between 1965 and 1975 in the ratio of the monthly payment on a fixed-payment mortgage to disposable income per household. The terms on typical house purchases and mortgage contracts in 1965 and 1975 are given in the first two columns of Table 1. The terms include, in descending order, the price of a fixed-quality house (the average new house purchased in 1967), an assumed 80 percent loan-to-value ratio, the implied downpayment and mortgage, the average term-to-maturity (which rose from twenty-five to twenty-seven years), the mortgage rate (which rose sharply from 5.75 to 8.75 percent), and the implied monthly payment (which rose from $115 to $276, an increase of 140 percent). To put the monthly payment for

TABLE 1

The Terms on Various Mortgage Contracts

	Typical 1965 Contract on New House	Typical 1975 Contract on New House	Graduated-Payment Contract (graduation rate = 4%) on 1975 New House
House price	$22,900	$42,900	$42,900
Loan-to-value	80%	80%	89%
Downpayment	$ 4,600	$ 8,600	$ 4,700
Mortgage	$18,300	$34,300	$38,200
Term-to-maturity	25 years	27 years	27 years
Mortgage rate	5.75%	8.75%	8.75%
Initial monthly payment	$115	$276	$210
Initial monthly payment adjusted for the growth in income per household	$115	$150	$114

Source: The house price, term-to-maturity, and mortgage rate data are from new homes financed by conventional mortgages and are published in the FHLBB Journal. The other data were supplied by the authors.

1975 in proper perspective, it is adjusted for the 84 percent growth in disposable income per household between 1965 and 1975 (the payment is divided by 1.84). This figure is up 30 percent from 1965, indicating that the monthly payment on a fixed-payment mortgage on a comparable new house is now nearly one and one-third times as large a proportion of current disposable income per household as it was in 1965.[3]

As the data in Table 1 indicate, inflation in housing prices raised the downpayment on a typical house by 84 percent between 1965 and 1975.[4] While disposable income per household rose proportionately, financial wealth did not keep pace with this increase. Because nominal, rather than real, yields are taxed, financial assets tend to earn negative real after-tax rates of return during inflationary periods;[5] even after taking into account the after-tax interest earned on financial instruments, the purchasing power of the instruments eroded. Households holding financial instruments are thus not able to meet higher nominal downpayment as quickly as they would have in the absence of inflation. Some households will even have to increase their saving rate in order ever to accumulate the rising required downpayment. Inflation and the downpayment requirement thus reduce the ability of households who have never owned houses to purchase their first homes.

In contrast to the erosion in the real after-tax rate of return

---

[3] For early calculations quite analagous to these, see Donald P. Tucker, "The Variable-Rate Graduated-Payment Mortgage," *Real Estate Review*, Spring 1975, pp. 73–74.

[4] It should be noted that an existing homeowner shifting from one home to another can make this increase in downpayment without hardship. If the price of a home purchased in 1965 rose by 60 percent (vis-à-vis the 85 percent increase in the price of new houses), then the sum of the capital gain, the cumulated equity built up through monthly payments, and the initial 20 percent downpayment in 1965 is sufficient for a 46 percent downpayment on the 1975 house. It is only first-home buyers who have been adversely affected in a significant way by the inflation of housing prices and increase in mortgage rates.

[5] The real after-tax return equals

$$R_a^r = (1 - t)R - \dot{p}^e,$$

where R is the nominal before-tax yield, t is the marginal tax rate of the investor, and $\dot{p}^e$ is the expected rate of inflation. To illustrate how inflation has reduced real after-tax returns, consider the following example. In 1965 the real after-tax return on a four-year Treasury note for an investor in the 25 percent tax bracket was, roughly,

$$1.5 = (1 - .25)4 - 1.5.$$

In 1975 the return was

$$-0.6 = (1 - .25)7.6 - 6.5.$$

And remember that inflation has also pushed investors into higher marginal tax brackets (raised t), which would reduce yields further.

on financial assets, the real after-tax rate of return on housing (the real implicit return in the form of housing services less maintenance costs and depreciation) need not necessarily decline during an inflationary period. Inflation thus favors housing investment relative to investment in financial assets.[6] Households that are able to pay the higher initial real monthly payments and purchase housing are able to take advantage of this higher relative rate of return. Moreover, they will accumulate real equity in their home faster than they would in a noninflationary environment. This occurs not because they pay off the mortgage principal faster—they do not—but because the nominal value of their house is rising with inflation; that is, the ratio of outstanding mortgage principal to the market value of the house (the loan-to-value ratio) is falling faster than it would in a noninflationary environment. Thus, the increase in monthly payments goes directly into real homeowner equity.

Inflation provides an additional benefit to homeowners who issue mortgages to finance their housing purchases. Even if the real rate of return on the housing investment remains unchanged, the real after-tax rate of return on homeowner equity increases. The difference between housing investment and homeowner equity is the amount of the housing investment that is financed with a mortgage. The return on the leveraged part of the housing investment is the real yield on housing less the real after-tax cost of mortgage financing. And the latter is reduced by inflation for a reason analogous to that which causes real after-tax yields on financial assets to fall—the tax deductibility of nominal, rather than real, mortgage payments.[7] Realizing that

---

[6] Federal tax laws also favor housing investment in several ways. First, and most important, is the exemption of the implicit housing services from taxation; in contrast, interest on financial instruments is taxed. Second, capital gains on the home are deferred until the home is sold, then taxed, if at all, at below the normal rate. (While this treatment of capital gains is not inappropriate, given that a large part of the gain is nominal, not real, the treatment does favor housing investment relative to investment in financial assets.)

[7] The real after-tax rate of return on homeowner equity is

$$Rhe = Rhous + \{Rhous - [(1-t)Rmor - \dot{p}^e]\}\frac{L}{V-L},$$

where Rhous is the real before- and after-tax rate of return on housing (implicit rent divided by the house price), Rmor is the home mortgage rate, t is the effective marginal tax rate of the homebuyer (t is thus the proportion of mortgage interest payments that can be deduced from federal tax payments), $\dot{p}^e$ is the expected inflation rate, L is the initial loan, and V is the initial house value. Rhous is the return on unleveraged housing investment; the second term is the net return on the leveraged portion of the investment. As noted above, Rhous should be independent of the expected inflation rate. In contrast, the return on the leveraged portion will rise in response to an increase in the expected inflation the real rate of return on housing is substantially higher than the real rate of return on savings accounts and other financial instruments during an inflationary environment, households will attempt to become homeowners as soon as possible. Some who would otherwise have rented indefinitely will purchase homes specifically because of this relatively higher real rate of return.

There are a variety of ways households that desire greater housing investment in response to inflation can meet the downpayment. Those with sufficient financial asset holdings may liquidate them. Another way is to borrow from other sources. Also, lenders who anticipate increasing house prices may acknowledge the decreased risk of their investment by lowering downpayment ratios. This has, in fact, occurred. The Federal Home Loan Bank Board (FHLBB) began liberalizing the regulations on loans with high loan-to-value ratios in 1971. The current (May 1978) regulations allow SLAS to invest up to 25 percent of their assets in loans in excess of 90 percent of a property's appraised value. Average loan-to-value ratios on conventional mortgages increased in the early 1970s in response to these liberalized regulations from about 74 percent to about 78 percent.

The cash-flow problem (the higher initial monthly payment) may also be addressed in several ways. Homeowners with substantial wealth in the form of savings accounts, securities, et cetera, may choose lower loan-to-value ratios than they otherwise would. This represents a change in the distribution of total initial wealth in favor of housing. And, by lowering monthly payments, larger downpayments lower the future rate of real homeowner equity accumulation.

Households that do not have this wealth may borrow from other sources to meet the higher current payments. One way to accomplish this is by issuing more consumer installment debt. This debt may directly finance consumer durables, but it simultaneously frees current income that may be devoted to the mortgage payment. The continuing increase in consumer debt is offset by the inflation-induced increase in homeowner equity on the households' balance sheets. Al-

---

rate unless Rmor rises by a full $1/(1-t)$ times the increase in the expected inflation rate.

Inflation tends to increase the real after-tax return on homeowner equity by substantial amounts. The returns in 1965 and 1975 were, assuming Rhous = 3.0, the loan-to-value and the mortgage rates in Table 1 and the tax and expected inflation rates in footnote 5:

$$1965 \quad 2.6 = 3 + \{3 - [.8(5.75) - 1.5]\}\,4$$
$$1975 \quad 15.8 = 3 + \{3 - [.8(8.75) - 6.5]\}\,4.$$

This phenomenal increase contrasts markedly with the decline in the real after-tax return on financial assets (see footnote 5).

ternatively, households may use that share of income which would otherwise be invested in savings accounts and other financial investments to meet the housing payment.

Finally, renting may be seen as a way to avoid the cash-flow burden. However, this escape route may be limited by the cash-flow burden of multifamily apartment owners who must pay the same high mortgage interest rate. Apartment owners could theoretically charge less than the current interest payment because they anticipate higher future rents. But, apartment owners must demonstrate to lenders that they can charge a rent sufficient to cover their mortgage payments and other expenses before the lenders will make the loans. Thus, if rents are not raised enough initially to cover the full impact of the increase in nominal rates on multifamily mortgages, a rise in the required downpayment on multifamily units results. Unless the multifamily owner is willing to raise the downpayment, rents on new units, like ownership payments, will rise with interest rates. Because existing units are close substitutes for new units, rents on existing units will also rise.

Homeowners can make numerous adjustments to the high mortgage rate and high rate of real homeowner equity accumulation during inflationary periods to achieve the same housing services, real rate of savings, and accumulation of wealth as in a noninflationary environment. This is not to suggest that they can adjust completely—there are some who undoubtedly cannot. Some homeowners may prefer a greater share of their savings in liquid instruments, for example, in spite of their eroding real value.

Graduated-Payment Mortgages

A proposed solution to the substantial increase in the downpayment and the initial monthly payment on the standard equal-payment mortgage is the graduated-payment mortgage (GPM). The latter mortgage would be like the former in that the interest rate and term-to-maturity would be fixed; it would differ in that monthly payments would be lower in the beginning but would then rise through time at the graduation rate. Because of the acceleration of inflation, nominal incomes are currently rising at a much faster rate, 8 percent annually, than the about 4 percent rate of the 1950s and early 1960s. It may be realistic to assume that this higher rate will continue. Thus, it is argued, borrowers can handle a 4 percent per annum rate of increase in their monthly mortgage payments as easily as they could handle the flat payments in the past; in both cases, their incomes would be rising at a rate 4 percentage points in excess of the rate of increase in their mortgage payments. Moreover, the buildup of *real* equity in their home progresses at the same rate with a 4 percent graduated-payment mortgage when the value of their house is inflating at 6 percent per year as it would with an equal-payment mortgage when house prices were inflating at 2 percent per year. Thus neither the foreclosure rates of lenders nor the likelihood of their taking losses on foreclosed houses would be higher on a graduated-payment mortgage in an inflationary environment than on a fixed-payment mortgage in a noninflationary environment.[8]

The third column in Table 1 indicates just how potent a graduated-payment mortgage can be. Given the same house price, interest rate, and term-to-maturity as is used in calculating the downpayment and initial monthly payment for the standard mortgage on a 1975 house, the graduated-payment contract can hold *both* the initial monthly payment as a proportion of household disposable income *and* the downpayment to the levels existing in 1965. Reducing the downpayment level to that of 1965 requires a decline in the downpayment ratio from 20 percent to 11 percent, and thus a rise in the mortgage from $34,300 to $38,200. In spite of this increase, the graduation in payments means that the initial monthly payment is $210, far below the $276 on a standard contract; after adjustment for the growth in income per household, the payment is the same as the initial payment in 1965.

Recognizing the benefits of the GPM, FHA requested and received experimental authority to insure GPMs under Section 245 of the Housing and Community Development Act of 1974, and issued regulations and implemented the program in November 1976. There are five types of GPMs insurable under this program:

PLAN I: Payments increase for five years at 2.5 percent per year

PLAN II: Payments increase for five years at 5.0 percent per year

PLAN III: Payments increase for five years at 7.5 percent per year

---

[8] The principal source of risk to lenders would appear to be a sharp long-term decline in the inflation rate and thus in the growth in nominal incomes. This would seem to create difficulties for those with graduated-payment streams. However, a sharp decline in the inflation rate would probably be accompanied by a significant fall in the mortgage rate. This would allow households to refinance the mortgage at a lower graduation rate in line with the now lower expected growth rate in income without raising their monthly payments.

PLAN IV: Payments increase for ten years at 2.0 percent per year

PLAN V: Payments increase for ten years at 3.0 percent per year

Although these plans cannot completely offset the impact of inflation in all circumstances, they do offer potential homebuyers who are prevented from homeownership by the cash-flow burden a significant advantage over the standard mortgage instrument.[9]

Summary

This chapter has explained the problems that high and rising interest rates cause for lenders and borrowers in the mortgage market. Maturity intermediation was seen to be an extremely risky venture for thrift institutions functioning in a competitive deposit market. The required accuracy of interest rate forecasting is well beyond the average capability of thrift institutions or market analysts, and portfolio restrictions may prevent thrifts from incorporating a fully anticipated rise in deposit costs into current mortgage rates.

Regarding borrowers, inflation premiums in lending rates raise required initial real debt payments and real equity accumulation for homebuyers financing their purchases with a standard fixed payment mortgage instrument. This creates a cash-flow problem. Moreover, inflation erodes the real purchasing power of financial assets even after allowing for interest earned because real after-tax returns tend to be negative during inflationary periods. Thus households have increased difficulty accumulating the required downpayment on their first home. The graduated-payment mortgage would assist in alleviating these financial problems. On the other hand, the higher real rate of return on homeowner equity relative to other investments favors homeownership, particularly for highly leveraged households. Thus the theoretical impact of inflation on the demand for homeownership is uncertain. The incredible boom in single family housing in recent years would seem to suggest that inflation has not reduced demand.

[9] Private lenders are also beginning to offer versions of GPMs on conventional mortgages. In a full page advertisement in the Midwest edition of the *Wall Street Journal* (June 23, 1977, p. 17), the Flip Mortgage Corporation describes a payment schedule where monthly payments rise by 50 percent over the first six years of the mortgage (an increase of 7 percent per year) and the ratio of the outstanding loan to the initial purchase price rises from 90 percent to 95 percent over the same period.

3

Direct Intervention
in the Mortgage Market

The federal government initiated its role in the home mortgage market when home mortgage lending came to a standstill in the Great Depression. The first federal action was the establishment of the Federal Home Loan Bank (FHLB) system as a central credit facility for the principal mortgage lenders, savings and loan associations. Other early efforts focused on reducing the risk and increasing the marketability of the mortgage instrument to renew the confidence of private mortgage lenders. Federal Housing Administration (FHA) default insurance for a standard fixed-payment mortgage and the creation of the Federal National Mortgage Association (FNMA) to aid in the establishment of a secondary market represent federal efforts to improve the efficiency of the mortgage market. The federal initiative has been expanded during the past decade to encompass substantial direct market intervention; FNMA has rapidly built up its mortgage holdings and the newly created Federal Home Loan Mortgage Corporation (FHLMC) has also acquired a significant mortgage portfolio. Moreover, efforts to reduce the risk and improve the marketability of investment in mortgages have been carried to their logical extreme in the creation of the Government National Mortgage Association (GNMA) guaranteed mortgage pools. The pools and FHLB loans to savings and loans are indirect sources of mortgage credit.

Although the goal of federal intervention remains unchanged—an increased supply of home mortgage credit—the increased emphasis on direct intervention and creation of the mortgage pools implies a change in the philosophy and goals of U.S. housing policy. Whereas early federal initiatives were aimed at increasing the allocation of funds to the mortgage market by making a poorly functioning mortgage market "efficient," the effect of recent direct intervention has

25

been to exploit institutional and regulatory rigidities in order to stimulate a greater quantity of mortgage credit than efficient markets would provide, and the guarantees have made mortgage investment as riskless and liquid as investment in any other private endeavor. Thus economic efficiency is now being sacrificed, rather than achieved, in the pursuit of housing goals presumed to be socially desirable. And this is in addition to the housing subsidy implicit in the federal tax code (see chapter 6, note 2).

An Overview of the Agencies: Their Actions and Objectives

Two federally sponsored credit agencies, the Federal National Mortgage Association (FNMA) and the Federal Home Loan Mortgage Corporation (FHLMC) supply credit to the home mortgage market directly. A number of on-budget agencies of the federal government also hold mortgages, but to a lesser degree. These include the Government National Mortgage Association, the Farmers Home Administration, and the Federal Housing and Veterans Administrations. The level of support by these agencies is indicated in Table 2. The on-budget agencies are aggregated into a federal category, and the total includes small holdings of the Federal Land Banks (FLB) accumulated in recent years ($0.6 billion during the 1973–1976 period).

FNMA responded to the 1966 liquidity crunch by increasing its mortgage holdings by 75 percent during the year. As can be seen, this growth has continued. The holdings of FNMA increased tenfold between 1965 and 1975, rising from $2.5 billion to $25.8 billion. While the rise has been monotonic, the rate of increase seems to have varied directly with movements in the home mortgage rate. The rise in the mortgage rate from 1965 to 1970 was accompanied by a rapid buildup of holdings, a rate of increase that slackened markedly between 1970 and 1972 when the mortgage rate fell. Again, FNMA net purchases accelerated in 1973 and 1974 in response to the increasing mortgage rate and slackened in 1975 when the rate stabilized. Net purchases by the FHLMC in recent years also appear to be related to the interest rate cycle, rising sharply in 1973 and particularly 1974, slowing down in 1975, and even turning negative in 1976. The holdings of on-budget agencies rose modestly between 1965 and 1969 and then declined gradually into early 1974. As a result of the Emergency Home Purchase Act of 1974, GNMA aggressively purchased mortgages for its own account during the rest of 1974 and 1975 and liquidated them in 1976. The total support for the home mortgage market increased by about $15 billion between 1965 and 1970, and by a similar amount between 1970 and 1976.

TABLE 2

HOLDINGS OF HOME MORTGAGES BY FEDERAL AGENCIES
(billions of dollars)

	1965	1966	1967	1968	1969	1970	1971	1972	1973	1974	1975	1976
FNMA (off-budget)	2.5	4.4	5.5	7.2	11.0	15.2	16.7	17.7	20.4	23.8	25.8	26.9
FHLMC (off-budget)	—	—	—	—	—	0.4	0.9	1.8	2.4	4.2	4.6	3.9
Federal (on-budget)	3.9	4.5	5.3	6.2	6.4	6.2	5.6	5.0	4.2	5.0	6.9	4.1
Total (including FLB)	6.4	8.9	10.8	13.4	17.4	21.8	23.2	24.5	27.1	33.4	37.8	35.5
Mortgage rate (percent)	5.81	6.25	6.46	6.97	7.81	8.45	7.74	7.60	7.95	8.92	9.01	9.00

SOURCE: Mortgage quantities are from various issues of the *Federal Reserve Bulletin*. The mortgage rate is the FHLBB series for conventional new homes and is published in the FHLBB *Journal*. The on-budget agencies include the Government National Mortgage Association, the Farmers Home Administration, and the Federal Housing and Veterans Administrations.

27

The growth in the two forms of indirect federal supply of mortgage credit, FHLB loans (advances) to savings and loan associations (SLAS) and mortgage pools, is indicated in Table 3. The net credit extended to SLAS consists of advances less equity that SLAS must hold in the FHLBS. The latter is approximately equal to 1 percent of each SLA's mortgage portfolio.

While advances to SLAS can support purchases of assets other than home mortgages, home mortgages have consistently accounted for three-quarters of total mortgage holdings and SLAS hold few assets other than mortgages and required liquid assets. Thus it is reasonable to assume that increases in advances largely support acquisitions of home mortgages. Two facts seem pertinent regarding advances. First, this form of federal support is even more strongly related to movements in interest rates than are other forms of support. This is indicated by the sharp increases in advances in 1969–1970 and 1973–1974 and particularly the declines in 1971 and 1975–1976.[1] Second, the repayment of advances, while significant, is never enough to lower the level to the previous trough. That is, there is a continual upward trend in this form of support as well as in the holdings of the other agencies. Neither of these facts should be particularly surprising. The demand by SLAS for advances is largely related to recent deposit flows; when inflows are heavy, SLAS repay loans, and when inflows slacken, SLAS borrow more. And significant periods of disintermediation (reduced deposit inflows) and reintermediation (extraordinarily large inflows) are related to movements in open-market interest rates relative to yields on deposits that are nearly constant, given deposit rate ceilings. The general growth in advances is also understandable in light of the growth in SLA total assets and the relatively low cost of advances.[2]

In recent years another indirect form of support for the home mortgage market has expanded rapidly. Since 1970, GNMA and FHLMC have been effectively issuing federally guaranteed securities to finance pools of home mortgages (the agencies guarantee the interest and

---

[1] The rise in advances in 1966 was limited by liquidity problems within the FHLB system. The system solved this problem by borrowing longer term in sufficient quantities to enable accumulation of short-term asset holdings. These holdings can be drawn down to make advances when the demand for such funds rises.

[2] Net advances were 5.1 percent of SLA assets at the end of 1965 and 4.8 percent at the end of 1976. The peak of this ratio, 9.4 percent, occurred at the end of 1974.

TABLE 3

Indirect Federal Holdings of Home Mortgages
(billions of dollars)

	1965	1966	1967	1968	1969	1970	1971	1972	1973	1974	1975	1976
Mortgage pools	0.1	0.5	1.0	1.4	1.8	3.0	7.3	10.7	14.8	20.1	30.0	43.9
SLA holdings	—	—	—	—	—	−1.0	−2.6	−4.0	−4.8	−5.7	−9.3	−10.6
Pools other than SLAs	0.1	0.5	1.0	1.4	1.8	2.0	4.7	7.6	10.0	14.4	20.7	33.3
Advances (net)	4.7	5.5	3.0	3.9	7.8	9.0	6.3	7.2	13.0	19.2	15.1	12.9
Pools other than SLAs plus advances (net)	4.8	6.0	4.0	5.3	9.6	11.0	11.7	14.8	23.0	33.6	35.8	46.2

SOURCES: Data on total mortgage pools and net advances (indebtedness of SLAs to FHLBS less equity of SLAs in FHLBS) are from the *Federal Reserve Flow of Funds Accounts*. Data on SLA holdings of mortgage pools for the 1973–1976 period are from various issues of the *Savings and Loan Fact Book*; earlier estimates have been constructed by the authors.

principal payments of the mortgages).[3] To the extent that the pools are held by institutions that would not have otherwise purchased home mortgages, such as insurance companies and pension funds, increases in the pools are equivalent to direct mortgage purchases. At the other extreme, if the securities are purchased by institutions that would otherwise have bought home mortgages, then the impact on the mortgage market is negligible. The outstanding pools have grown from $3 billion in 1970 (these were largely guaranteed by the Farmers Home Administration) to $44 billion in 1976. A reasonable working assumption is that the funds that SLAS invest in pools would have been invested in home mortgages anyway, because SLAS are so limited in their investment possibilities, but that funds invested by others would have been invested in low-risk agency or corporate bonds, because these institutions (mutual savings banks, pension funds, and insurance companies) hold large amounts of such assets. An estimate of the home mortgage pools not held by SLAS is given in Table 3.

The sum of advances (net) and pools other than those held by SLAS is a measure of the credit extended indirectly by the agencies. As can be seen in the last row of Table 3, the growth in this form of support of the home mortgage market has been phenomenal, rising from $12 billion to $46 billion between 1971 and 1976.

The data in Table 4 attempt to put the federal support of the home mortgage market into perspective. The first row combines the direct and indirect mortgage holdings of the agencies (the total row of Table 2 and the last row of Table 3). The second row is the stock of outstanding home mortgages, and the last row is the fraction of the outstanding stock supported by the agencies. In 1965, federal support amounted to only 5 percent; by the middle 1970s the support was up to 15 percent.[4] The jump was largely limited to two periods, 1968–1970 and 1972–1974, when interest rates rose sharply.[5]

---

[3] FHLMC actually issues securities; GNMA simply guarantees the mortgage pools themselves. The securities/pools are issued in denominations of $25,000. The rationale for the high denomination is probably the same as that for the minimum $10,000 denomination in which Treasury bills are sold—to prohibit depositors with limited financial wealth from shifting out of deposits.

[4] A more conservative estimate is obtained by assuming that only three-quarters of net advances and mortgage pools other than those held by SLAS constitute support of the home mortgage market. The ratio of direct plus 75 percent of indirect support to total mortgage debt also tripled between 1965 and 1975, rising from .045 to .135.

[5] For a full discussion of the growth in federal support of this market, see Leo Grebler, "The Role of the Public Sector in Residential Financing," *Resources for Housing*, Proceedings of the First Annual Conference, FHLB of San Francisco, 1975, pp. 67–116.

TABLE 4

DIRECT AND INDIRECT FEDERAL HOLDINGS OF HOME MORTGAGES AS A FRACTION OF THE MORTGAGE MARKET
(billions of dollars)

	1965	1966	1967	1968	1969	1970	1971	1972	1973	1974	1975	1976
(1) Direct plus indirect federal support	11.2	14.9	14.8	18.7	27.0	32.8	34.2	39.3	50.1	67.0	73.6	81.6
(2) Stock of home mortgages	218.3	231.6	245.0	262.1	280.2	294.6	323.2	365.8	412.2	446.7	487.4	551.9
(1) ÷ (2)	.05	.06	.06	.07	.10	.11	.11	.11	.12	.15	.15	.15

SOURCE: Row (1) is the sum of the total row of Table 2 and the last row of Table 3. The data on the stock of home mortgages are from the *Federal Reserve Flow of Funds Accounts*.

Recent testimony on the Financial Reform Act of 1976 in the House renewed interest in the role these agencies should play. Both the objectives and the ultimate impacts of these agencies are difficult to pinpoint, a fact that intensifies the controversy surrounding their operations. The objectives of the enabling legislation for the agency activities are explored in the following sections. The institutional arrangements by which the agencies function are then measured against these objectives. The last part of this section deals with the impact of these activities on mortgage rates, credit, and housing outlays.

The FNMA. The Federal National Mortgage Association was created in the 1930s to aid the establishment of a national secondary market for FHA mortgages. Congress always intended the secondary mortgage market facility to be privately owned. But because of the financial risks involved, there were no private initiatives in response to the initial FHA legislation in 1935. The federally sponsored FNMA secondary market facility was chartered in 1938 with the view of eventual private ownership. The agency gradually took on additional responsibilities and operations as a result of the Serviceman's Readjustment Act of 1948 and the Housing and Urban Development (HUD) Act of 1954, but these other operations were spun off in 1968, leaving a new private FNMA with only the secondary market facility.

The secondary market facility was made private because it served and benefited private financial institutions, particularly mortgage bankers. There was no long-term need for federal involvement, because the users of the secondary market service have always been willing to pay for the service. At the same time, the private FNMA operations serve the public interest by providing liquidity to the mortgage instrument.

Congress indicated very strongly in the original legislation the intent that FNMA be a "dealer" in mortgages, but not an investor in competition with private mortgage investors. Section 304(a)(1) of the Charter Act specifically provides: "the volume of the Corporation's purchases and sales . . . should be determined by the Corporation from time to time . . . *as will reasonably prevent excessive use of the Corporation's facility*" [italics added].[6] In spite of this safeguard, the FNMA, for one reason or another, has for the most part been a net purchaser of mortgages. The following statement taken from HUD's

---

[6] National Housing Act, section 304(a)(1); 12 U.S.C. 1719 (a)(1).

1972 budget illustrates why the facility accumulated mortgages in its early years:

> During World War II, it [FNMA] was primarily interested in providing necessary credit for war housing, without great concern for whether the mortgages were potentially saleable on the private market. Similarly, in the postwar period, a primary purpose was to provide quickly a large volume of credit for housing veterans. It purchased FHA-insured and VA-guaranteed mortgages with minimum regard to whether there was a reasonable early prospect of their resale at the prices for which they were purchased. Meanwhile, as the FHA undertook to assist special classes of housing such as cooperatives, housing in Alaska, and housing near military installations, so did the FNMA.[7]

Congress resisted the trend to a large net volume of purchases by reaffirming its intention of maintaining the "dealer" status of the secondary market facility with enactment of the FNMA Charter Act of 1954. The FNMA was rechartered into a three-part corporation in an attempt to separate those activities that required mortgage investment from the secondary market facility. The facility was, as a result of this legislation, to relinquish its role as an investor. During the second half of the 1950s, FNMA accumulated some mortgages, but it liquidated them during the first half of the 1960s. Total holdings were only around $2 billion in 1965. The sharp reduction in the availability of private mortgage credit in 1966 marked a turning point in secondary market activity, however. In the next five years holdings grew at an average annual rate of about 35 percent, rising to $15 billion. This growth rate has declined to about 15 percent during the past five years, but net purchases in absolute terms have increased. By the end of 1975, FNMA's portfolio of home mortgages exceeded $25 billion.

Although amendments in 1968 and 1974 required FNMA to *purchase* mortgages for low and moderate income families through various arrangements with GNMA, the initial cautions against excessive use of the secondary market facility are still part of FNMA's charter. Further evidence that the facility was to remain a dealer is obtained in section 301, Title III, of the National Housing Act. This section indicates that the goal of the secondary market facility is to "provide supplementary assistance to the secondary market for home mortgages by providing *a degree of liquidity* for mortgage investments,

---

[7] Department of Housing and Urban Development, Summary of Budget Authorizations and Expenditures for Fiscal Year 1972, Office of the Secretary, January 1971.

thereby improving the distribution of investment capital available for home mortgage financing" [italics added].[8] This suggests that strict adherence to the Charter Act would prohibit substantial mortgage investment and raises the issue of why the FNMA portfolio has grown so rapidly since 1965.

Two separate explanations are required, one for the period before FNMA became public in 1968, and another for the period since 1968. The growth during the earlier period largely reflected the combined forces of rising mortgage rates and the FNMA auction procedure. Prior to 1968, FNMA established an administered price at which it would buy mortgages and another price at which it would sell. These prices were typically set with a lag, partly because of administrative procedures and partly because FNMA felt that this lag helped stabilize interest rates. Because rates rose (prices fell) fairly continuously during this period, the FNMA "buy" price was generally above the market price, and the sell price below market. Beginning in 1968 FNMA introduced the Free Market Auction System. The current practice is for FNMA to receive offers for commitments at its biweekly auctions and then determine the volume of commitments to accept. Consequently, FNMA can control its long-run growth rate fairly accurately.

A guide to the desired future growth of FNMA is the proposal the FNMA Corporate Planning Department made in late 1976 to the FNMA board of directors that the FNMA continue to accumulate mortgages as long as their yields exceed the FNMA's cost of funds.[9] (This is what might be expected from a profit-maximizing institution.) The question of FNMA growth then becomes a question of what determines the spread between mortgage yields and the FNMA cost of funds and how this spread is likely to change as FNMA grows. The low cost of FNMA debt issues is discussed below; how the cost is affected by substantial debt issues is considered in chapter 8 in the discussion of the federalization of the mortgage market.

FNMA's most important advantage in the debt market is the perception of investors that the default risk of FNMA debt is close to zero. This perception is probably accurate, but not because FNMA has a high rating in measures of risk, such as the debt-equity ratio, usually applied to private corporations. FNMA is highly leveraged and therefore extremely risky by these standards. Rather, the perception reflects FNMA's origins as a public agency and the awareness that the federal

---

[8] National Housing Act, Title III—National Mortgage Associations, Public Law 479, 73rd Congress, 48 Stat. 1246, 12 U.S.C. 1701.

[9] "FNMA's Financial Goals," Office of Corporate Planning, April 12, 1976, unpublished report of the FNMA.

government is not likely to let FNMA fail. FNMA operates the secondary mortgage market facility, providing a dealer function for HUD as well as private mortgage originators. Moreover, the secretary of HUD has broad regulatory authority over FNMA, and federal regulators have always been extremely reluctant to allow regulated firms to fail, especially when they are large, visible, and important to the entire mortgage banking and housing industries. A second advantage enjoyed by FNMA in the capital market is the special status of FNMA debt as legal investments for federally supervised institutions.[10] In this capacity, FNMA securities can be counted as meeting SLA liquidity requirements and used as collateral for FHLB and Federal Reserve advances; they can be used to meet pledging requirements against government deposits at banks; they can be employed by the Federal Reserve in its open market operations; and so forth. It is noteworthy that although FNMA is private, its ability to intermediate in the capital markets derives from its federal sponsorship and federally granted privileges. It was for this reason that Congress maintained federal regulation of FNMA when it made the corporation private.

The GNMA. The Government National Mortgage Association (GNMA) was created in 1968 to assume the management and liquidation and special assistance functions previously carried out by FNMA. The special assistance function involves purchase of below-market rate mortgages under various sections of the National Housing Act. These mortgages are then typically sold to FNMA on the private market at a market price. Because the private market requires a market rate of return, the mortgages are sold at a price below par. The loss to GNMA is financed by congressional appropriations. The procedure of GNMA buying and then selling to FNMA is known as the Tandem Plan, because the institutions are acting in tandem.

The GNMA tandem program was initially perceived as a means of maintaining high levels of subsidized housing starts during periods of rising mortgage rates. When mortgage market conditions tightened in the summer of 1971, for instance, the discount on FHA 7 percent home mortgages widened to a range of eight to ten points (the price fell to ninety to ninety-two).[11] Reducing the discount required an increase in the FHA ceiling rate, a move that is always politically

---

[10] FNMA is also only one of two (the other is FHLBS) privately owned corporations that benefit from a "Treasury Backstop Authority" which authorizes the secretary of the Treasury to purchase up to $2¼ billion of FNMA obligations at any one time.

[11] A full discussion of FHA ceiling rates, "points," and their impact is given in chapter 4.

unattractive. It was felt that a rise in the FHA coupon ceiling rate and/or an increase in the points charged the borrower would slow the ongoing boom in subsidized construction. In order to avoid a housing crunch, GNMA implicitly "paid" the points by buying the mortgages at par and selling them at a discount.

By 1974, the tandem program was perceived as a major counter-cyclical housing tool. In January, GNMA was authorized to purchase 200,000 FHA/VA 7.75 percent mortgages. In May, the purchase of another 100,000 FHA/VA mortgages was authorized, this time at a rate of 8 percent. GNMA sold these mortgages at a price averaging about five points less than they paid. The tandem program was expanded to the conventional mortgage market with the passage of the Emergency Home Purchase Act of 1974. As a result, the current tandem program has the capability to subsidize the demand for mortgage credit and simultaneously act as a vehicle to provide additional mortgage funds during a housing downturn. GNMA increased its holdings of home mortgages by almost $3½ billion in 1974, 1975, and early 1976 and has since liquidated them. There is, however, one undesirable aspect of the tandem programs, that being the giving of the commitments to builders rather than directly to households. The supply of commitments in any given market area is likely to be limited to only one, or at most several builders. Builders without commitments may be forced to cut prices to reduce excess inventories, whereas the builder with the commitment lowers the effective cost without cutting price. Thus, some of the value of the below-market interest rate accrues to builders, rather than to homebuyers.

In addition to operating the tandem program, GNMA has been instrumental in creating an extremely successful new mortgage instrument, the pass-through mortgage-backed security. GNMA guarantees timely principal and interest payment on these securities, but does not hold the mortgages directly. Almost all of the pass-through securities have been issued by mortgage bankers who originate and service the mortgages. The mortgage banker is responsible to GNMA for the interest and principal payments, regardless of the experience of the pool. GNMA limits its risk exposure by establishing capital requirements for participating mortgage bankers and requiring them to hold reserves with GNMA.

Beginning in the summer of 1975, the Chicago Board of Trade implemented a futures market for GNMA pass-through securities. A GNMA future is the right to buy a GNMA security for a specified price at a specified date in the future. This market, which has been extremely active, provides thrift institutions, mortgage bankers, and other originators of mortgages with a vehicle to hedge against the interest rate risk associated with origination. For example, a mortgage banker may obtain a forward commitment from a dealer to underwrite a GNMA pass-through in three months. If mortgage rates fall in the interim, the mortgages he originates for the pool will be valued below par, and the mortgage banker will be forced to absorb the capital loss. He can hedge this loss by selling mortgage interest rate futures contracts. The price of these contracts will fall with the price of his mortgages in the pool; thus the mortgage banker can buy back the futures contract at a profit, offsetting the loss on the mortgage pool.[12] It is worth noting that the short-term horizon of the market prevents thrifts from using it to shift the interest rate risk associated with their investment of short-term deposits in long-term mortgages.

The FHLB and FHLMC. The Federal Home Loan Bank system is yet another product of the Great Depression, created to provide liquidity to a fundamentally illiquid savings and loan industry. Many SLAs failed during these depression years, including many sound institutions with insufficient liquidity. Commercial banks had provided liquidity prior to this, but when faced with a serious liquidity shortage of their own, they were in no position to assist the SLA industry. The advances mechanism of the Home Loan Banks—which have backup authority to borrow from the Federal Reserve System—filled the liquidity void. The level of advances is largely determined by deposit flows. When inflows are large (1971–1972, 1975–1976) advances are repaid; when inflows are small (1969, 1973–1974) advances are built up.

The FHLBs receive no federal appropriations and therefore rely exclusively on income from advances to cover borrowing and administrative costs and to earn a return on equity. Prior to 1970 the system charged its average borrowing cost on its outstanding stock of advances (plus a small markup). Since then the rate on advances has often (1970–1972 and 1975) been set about a half percentage point below the average cost of funds. This has been achieved by a conscious decision to forgo return on equity. Because FHLBs are owned by member SLAs, the decision to lend at below-market rates amounts to a subsidy from institutions (their borrowers and depositors) that borrow relatively less to those that borrow relatively more.

The two periods of below-cost lending are instructive. In April 1970 the FHLBs began to offer one-year fixed-term advances at a cost 25 to 75 basis points below the cost of funds. The stated purpose of

---

[12] For a discussion of the operation of this market, see Richard Sandor, "Trading Mortgage Interest-Rate Futures," FHLB *Journal*, September 1975, pp. 2–9.

this subsidy was to discourage the expected repayment of advances in response to anticipated deposit inflows. Further steps were taken in November 1970 to limit repayments. This program has been estimated to have induced SLAs to purchase $2½ billion more in home mortgages between the second quarter of 1970 and the first quarter of 1971 (and $2½ billion less in the following year) than they otherwise would have. The second episode was initiated in May 1974 when $3½ billion of five-year advances were made at 50 to 80 basis points below the cost of five-year issues. This subsidy program was billed as a response to the 1974 housing slump. The estimate here is that SLAs purchased $1½ billion more of mortgages during the first half of 1974 (and $1½ billion less in the first half of 1976) than they otherwise would have. The decision to encourage (subsidize) borrowing during a downturn in housing cycles, such as occurred in early 1970 and 1974, seems quite consistent with the stated objectives of the FHLB Board to stabilize "residential construction and financing in periods when monetary or financial conditions create a dearth of mortgage money."[13]

In June 1978, a third below-cost lending program was announced. Under this program up to $2 billion a year for ten years will be advanced to thrifts that "demonstrate leadership in revitalizing urban housing" at 50 basis points below the FHLB's borrowing cost. This Community Investment Fund is part of the Carter administration's urban program. Rather than using direct tax dollars to subsidize mortgage lending in older urban neighborhoods, other borrowers and depositors are subsidizing this lending through higher charges on their loans and lower returns on their savings.

The Federal Home Loan Mortgage Corporation (FHLMC) was established in 1970 to purchase conventional mortgages from SLAs with the intent of improving the liquidity of the SLA mortgage portfolio. Since that time, FNMA has also been authorized to purchase conventional mortgages, resulting in overlapping authority in this area. The FHLMC steadily accumulated home mortgages through 1975, with their portfolio reaching a peak of $4½ billion. In 1976 they liquidated over a half billion dollars. While the willingness of FHLMC to reduce its holdings during a single family housing boom contrasts with FNMA behavior, the reduction is quite modest. The rationale for the apparent desire of FHLMC to maintain a mortgage portfolio may be analogous to that underlying the behavior of FNMA. Because mortgage rates exceed the average borrowing costs of FNMA and FHLMC main-

---

[13] *Savings and Loan Fact Book*, United States League of Savings Associations, Chicago, 1976, p. 94.

38

taining a portfolio is profitable. Moreover, these profits, as well as most of the servicing and origination fees, accrue to savings and loans which effectively own the FHLMC and sell the mortgages to FHLMC initially.

The Impact of the Agencies on Interest Rates, Credit Flows, and Housing

The severe cycles of housing construction during the past decade have been attributed primarily to periodic shortages of mortgage credit. Prior to 1966, efforts to increase the supply of mortgage credit focused on smoothing the flow of funds to the mortgage market by providing liquidity both to mortgage lending institutions (FHLB) and to the mortgage instrument (FNMA) and by reducing the risk of mortgage investment (FHA). The goal of these policies was to improve the efficiency of the mortgage market so that it could attract a competitive market share of existing savings. The large and continued accumulation of mortgages under federal auspices since 1966 suggests that the intent of policy has shifted to diverting a greater than competitive market share of savings to housing in an attempt to achieve the legislated housing goal, embodied in the Housing and Urban Development Act of 1968, of adding 26 million new or rehabilitated housing units to the nation's housing stock by 1978.[14]

The impact of agency activities on home mortgages flows and residential construction expenditures is the subject of much debate. At one extreme are those who contend that, because credit rationing is so pervasive in the home mortgage market, agency mortgage purchases induce a like increase in household mortgage supply and housing expenditures. At the other extreme are those who contend that, because funds flow freely from one market to another, the increase in agency mortgage market support will have no impact either on these quantities or on relative interest rates. At issue is the extent to which issues of securities by agencies to finance purchases of home mortgages ultimately induce other sectors to invest less, freeing up resources for housing production.

The prospects of other sectors sharply reducing their ultimate credit demands in response to small increases in borrowing rates are slim. Governments continue to borrow to finance operating deficits, for example. While business firms do shift their borrowing pattern somewhat to minimize total borrowing costs, their total borrowing is

[14] Housing and Urban Development Act of 1968, Public Law 90-448, 82 Stat. 476, 601 12 U.S.C. 1701 and 42 U.S.C. 1441a.

reduced by much less than the agency security issues. The extent to which agency intermediation "crowds out" other borrowers depends on the relative elasticities of the supply of mortgages vis-à-vis the supply of other securities. Empirical estimates indicate that the corporate demand for funds is much less elastic than household demand. State and local government demand appears to be moderately less elastic, while U.S. government borrowing is totally inelastic with respect to interest rates. These relative elasticities suggest that agency mortgage market purchases will result in only marginal increases in the total supply of mortgage credit, primarily at the expense of state and local governments.

This hypothesis is consistent with the results of simulations of a flow-of-funds model reported by Hendershott and Villani.[15] These results imply that, for every $1 billion infusion of mortgage credit by agencies, $850 million "leaks" from the mortgage market. Through a series of complex portfolio adjustments by many investors, the financial system channels these funds to the market for agency securities. This decrease of $150 million in the borrowing by other sectors is achieved only by a substantial increase in the borrowing rates of these sectors.

What do these results imply for the net impact of direct federal credit market intervention on the mortgage and housing stock during the past decade? Net federal support for the home mortgage market increased by over $42 billion between 1965 to the end of 1975. This accumulation is estimated to have increased the stock of home mortgages by just less than $7 billion (.15 times $42 billion). Given a loan-to-value ratio of .75, the stock of housing increased by about $10 billion as a result of the federal support. And if the loan-to-value ratio increases, as might be expected, the increase is even less. To put this impact in better perspective, the household housing stock has recently been valued at nearly a trillion dollars by the Department of Commerce.[16] Thus, agency activity increased the housing stock by about 1 percent in the past decade.

The finding that agencies had a relatively small impact on the total quantity of mortgage credit suggests that other mortgage investors must have left the market. Not surprisingly, it was less

---

[15] Patric H. Hendershott and Kevin E. Villani, "The Federally Sponsored Credit Agencies, Their Behavior and Impact," in R. Buckley, J. Tuccillo, and K. Villani, eds., *Capital Markets and the Housing Sector: Perspectives on Financial Reform* (Cambridge, Mass.: Ballinger Publishing Company, 1977), pp. 291–309.

[16] John C. Musgrave, "Fixed Nonresidential Business and Residential Capital in the United States, 1925–75," *Survey of Current Business*, April 1976, Table 6, p. 51.

restricted investors, such as life insurance companies (LICS), private pension funds (PPFS), and mutual savings banks (MSBS), that shifted into other assets. These portfolio shifts are illustrated in Figure 2 which contains the shares of home mortgages held by various institutions. The share held by LICS and PPFS has fallen throughout the past two decades, but the decline during the last decade was significantly more precipitous. The decline during the earlier decade is primarily attributable to the more rapid asset growth of SLAS, a captive of the mortgage market. Portfolio shifting accounted for a smaller share; the percentage of total LIC and PPF assets invested in home mortgages fell only slightly from 18 percent in 1956 to about 14 percent in 1966. During the decade the two institutions accumulated $15 billion in home mortgages.

With the accelerated growth of agencies (and mortgage pools) beginning in 1966, LICS and PPFS literally abandoned the home mortgage market. During the 1966–1975 decade their aggregate holdings fell back to the 1955 level. The switch in mortgage holdings from LICS and PPFS to agencies is illustrated vividly in Figure 2. The combined share of the federally sponsored credit agencies, including the pools, and the private discretionary investors remained roughly constant at 17 percent of the market between 1965 and 1975, but the relative share of agencies has increased sharply from 2 percent to 12 percent.

The other discretionary sector whose behavior changed sharply around the middle 1960s is mutual savings banks. During the 1956–1965 period over 70 percent of the increase in their assets was in the form of home mortgages; during the 1966–1975 decade this percentage fell to 32 percent.

The relative shift of discretionary investors out of home mortgages was a rational response to a decline in the relative yield on mortgages induced by the agency purchases. The impact of agencies on the home mortgage rate can be illustrated with reference to the spread between the home mortgage rate and the corporate bond rate plotted in Figure 3. The average spread, which oscillated around 1⅓ percentage points during the 1956–1965 period, fell to zero by 1971, and has since fluctuated around this low level. The historical spread was due to the servicing costs and default-risk and marketability premiums built into home mortgage rates. Timothy Q. Cook considered numerous possible explanations for the fall in the rate spread, including changes in the risk, marketability, and servicing costs.[17]

---

[17] Timothy Q. Cook, "The Residential Mortgage Market in Recent Years," *Economic Review*, FRB of Richmond, September/October 1974, pp. 3–18.

FIGURE 2

Relative Shares of Home Mortgages Outstanding Held by Various Sectors, 1957 to 1975

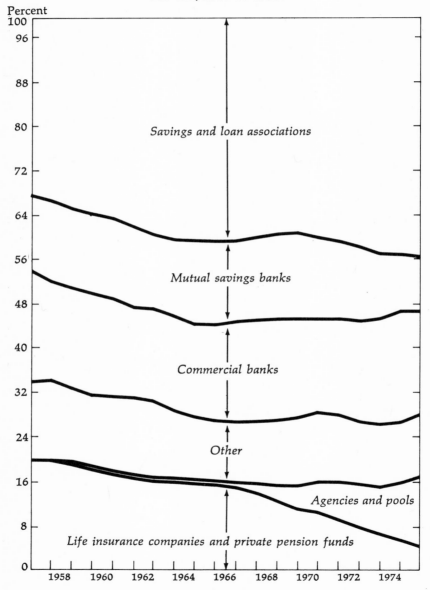

SOURCE: *Federal Reserve System, Flow of Funds Accounts, 1945–1972*; and *Flow of Funds Accounts, 2d Quarter 1976.*

FIGURE 3

Observed and Adjusted Spreads between Home Mortgage and Corporate Bond Rates

(percentage points)

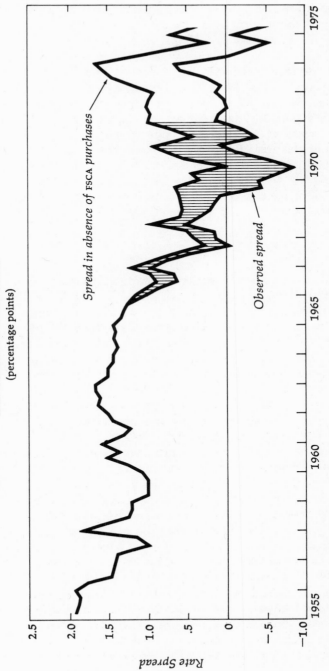

SOURCE: Reproduced from Patric H. Hendershott, *Understanding Capital Markets, Volume 1: A Flow-of-Funds Financial Model* (Lexington, Mass.: Lexington Books, 1977), p. 242.

43

He concludes that increased mortgage purchases of sponsored agencies were probably the principal cause.

The Hendershott and Villani model simulations support Cook's hypothesis. Agency mortgage purchases are calculated as having reduced the spread between the yields on home mortgages and corporate bonds by 87 basis points, or approximately two-thirds of the observed decline. This impact on the interest rate differential is indicated in Figure 3 by the hatched area. In the absence of the activities of the agencies, the mortgage rate would have been at the upper bound of the area; the observed rate is the lower bound. While the estimated impact of the agencies on the home mortgage rate may be on the high side, it seems clear that the agencies have reduced the home mortgage rate by at least a half percentage point from what it would have been in the absence of the expansion in their activities.

Summary

Federal participation in the home mortgage market has grown substantially during the past decade. The percentage of the stock of home mortgages effectively held by the federal government and its sponsored agencies rose from 5 percent in 1965 to 15 percent in 1975. Federal supply of home mortgage credit takes three general forms: (1) direct mortgage purchases by FNMA, FHLMC, and GNMA; (2) indirect purchases of SLAs financed by advances (loans) from the FHLBS; and (3) indirect purchases of institutions other than SLAs induced by the federal guaranteeing of mortgage pools. In the second half of the 1960s, the increased federal role was due to growth in FNMA; in the 1970s the mortgage pools have constituted the primary federal impetus. Advances have exhibited a strong cyclical movement around a trend approximating the growth rate of total home mortgage debt.

The growth of the sponsored agencies, particularly FNMA, is not called for in their charters. The primary cause of the growth appears to be the monetary reward to be gained. Because FNMA can borrow at virtually the risk-free Treasury rate, borrowing and investing in mortgages is profitable. It is profitable both for FNMA shareholders and for mortgage bankers who originate and service most of the mortgages FNMA purchases. One interpretation of the recent buildup of FHLMC's holdings (and the upward trend in the level of advances) is that SLAs, too, decided to participate in this sure thing. The implicit profits of FHLMC indirectly accrue to them, and they also sell the mortgages to FHLMC, earning the origination and servicing fees. The reason why these organizations are allowed to violate the intent, if not the exact wording, of their charters and are allowed to use their special status as federal agencies to reap profits for themselves and their constituencies is uncertain. However, a likely explanation, or at least a prerequisite to the continuation, of these activities is the prohousing bias of the relevant congressional committees—Banking, Housing, and Urban Affairs in the Senate and Banking, Finance, and Urban Affairs in the House. This same bias would explain why the extraordinary growth in the mortgage pools has not been questioned.

The most obvious impact of the agencies has been the reduction in the home mortgage rate relative to other rates and the consequent shift of discretionary investors—life insurance companies, pension funds, and mutual savings banks to some extent—out of the home mortgage market. Given this shift, the increase in total mortgage credit has been far less than the increase in that supplied by the agencies (one estimate is only 15 percent). While there has almost certainly been some positive stimulus to housing, the magnitude has apparently not been large. In our view, as developed in chapter 6, the primary impact of the creeping federalization of the home mortgage market has been a gain (lower mortgage rate) for homeowners who would have purchased their homes in the absence of the agency actions and a loss (lower deposit rate) for depositors. On the other hand, the cyclical lending of FHLBS to SLAS has obviously played an important and necessary (in our regulated financial system) role for housing.

4

Usury Laws and FHA/VA
Rate Ceilings

State usury ceilings on mortgage rates and ceiling rates on FHA/VA mortgages reflect a continuing tradition of borrower protection. The argument of usury rate ceiling proponents has changed little over the past several thousand years; only the zealousness with which it is embraced has diminished. The rise in open-market interest rates in the late 1960s and the reluctance of policy makers to raise the ceilings has increased their importance relative to earlier years. The rationale of the ceilings established by state governments and by FHA/VA and the impact of the ceilings on mortgage interest rates and fund flows are discussed in this chapter.

State Usury Laws

Usury ceilings on mortgage rates are imposed by about one-third of all states.[1] The level of these rates varies widely between states. It appears that many state legislatures attempt to set the ceiling at the high end of the range of mortgage rates existing when the legislation is being enacted. Unfortunately, mortgage rates have changed much more rapidly than state legislatures could respond. Moreover, the political will to respond has been weakened by the overtones of consumer protection that inevitably shroud the existing ceiling level.

The theoretical case against usury ceilings is clear. When they are successful in reducing the effective cost of mortgage credit, they create an excess demand for mortgage loans. Borrowers with substantial wealth and income can make large percentage downpayments and can live with shorter-term loans. These terms are the most at-

---

[1] N. M. Bowsher, "Usury Laws: Harmful When Effective," *Review*, FRB of St. Louis, August 1974, pp. 16–23.

tractive to lenders and thus such borrowers will continue to obtain mortgage credit. They may even pay less as a result of the ceiling. But high-risk borrowers, typically characterized by little wealth and/or low income, will be unable to secure mortgage credit at the usury ceiling. Moreover, where it is legal to do so, lenders will raise the effective mortgage interest rate above the ceiling by charging points or closing fees of various sorts at the time the mortgage is made.

A point is equal to 1 percent of the value of the mortgage. A typical rule of thumb used by lenders is to charge two points for each quarter point the coupon yield is below the market yield. Assume for the sake of illustration that a usury law constrains the coupon yield on a new mortgage to 1¼ percent below the market rate, and thus the lender charges ten points.[2] Ten points on a $40,000 mortgage requires a $4,000 payment to the lender at closing. From the lender's viewpoint he is making a $36,000 loan ($40,000 less the $4,000 payment) but will receive the monthly payments implied by a $40,000 loan. This clearly raises the effective rate of return on the mortgage. How much the rate is raised depends on how soon the mortgage is repaid (and what the quoted mortgage rate is). If the mortgage is repaid at the end of a single year, for example, then the lender receives approximately 11 percent extra (roughly four thousand, the value of the points, divided by thirty-six thousand, the value of the effective loan). If the loan is repaid after two years, then the $4,000 in income must be spread over two years and the impact on the percentage rate of return is less. Table 5 shows the impact on the effective interest rate paid by a borrower charged ten front-end points on a thirty-year mortgage under different assumptions regarding the years to repayment and mortgage (coupon) rate paid.

The use of points to raise the effective yield is somewhat limited by "public relations" and, in some cases, law. To the extent that the ceiling prevents discretionary lenders from obtaining a risk-adjusted market rate of return, these lenders will shift their funds into other investments. Thus a decline in mortgage lending is expected. Moreover, even if lenders did charge enough points to raise the effective rate to the market rate, a reduction in mortgage lending would be expected. While the effective loan rate would be the same, borrowers would be faced with higher effective downpayments. In our example, if the points were paid by the borrower and if the regular downpay-

---

[2] This is usually said to be based on an average mortage life of twelve years. When mortgage rates are about 5 percent a twelve-year assumed life would result in the rule of thumb.

TABLE 5
EFFECTIVE BORROWING COSTS FOR A MORTGAGE INITIALLY DISCOUNTED
BY TEN POINTS UNDER DIFFERENT REPAYMENT AND
MORTGAGE RATE ASSUMPTIONS

	Assumed Mortgage Coupon Rate		
Year-end Repaid	6%	7½%	9%
1st	17.004	18.579	20.158
2nd	11.697	13.269	14.846
4th	9.062	10.636	12.215
8th	7.770	9.349	10.935
12th	7.362	8.946	10.539
20th	7.082	8.676	10.280
30th	7.013	8.612	10.222

SOURCE: Computer simulations of effective yields on a new thirty-year mortgage purchased at 90 percent of par, courtesy of GNMA.

ment were 9 percent—$4,000 on a $44,000 home—then he would have had to come up with $8,000—$4,000 for the downpayment and $4,000 in points—at the time of purchase. If the points are paid by the seller or the builder and passed through to the buyer in the form of a higher purchase price, then the 9 percent downpayment would rise from $4,000 to $4,320 (and the mortgage would rise to $43,680).[3] The higher downpayment reduces the demand for housing and hence for mortgage credit.

The data in Table 5 also illustrate that the effective rate on a mortgage with points is much higher for the short-term buyer than the long-term buyer. In the example, the borrower who repaid a 7½ percent mortgage originally issued at a ten point discount (issued when the market rate was 8¾ percent) in twenty years ended up paying an effective rate of 8.68 percent, 7 basis points less than the original market new issue rate. In contrast, a borrower who repaid in four years would pay 10.64 percent, or almost 2 percentage points above the initial 8¾ percent going market rate. Thus the use of points causes arbitrary income transfers between households. In addition, points reduce labor mobility. Because early repayment of a mortgage with 10 points raises the effective borrowing rate—by more than 11

[3] This is, of course, preferable to the alternative effective downpayment of $8,000. It is difficult to imagine that most of the points would not be passed through to the buyer, and to the extent that they fall on the seller, he is less able to purchase another house.

percentage points if repaid within a year—people with recent high-point mortgages would be less willing to relocate than if they had not been charged points.

Table 5 also illustrates the nonlinear relationship between points charged and coupon rates. The lender rule of thumb—two discount points for 25 basis points in yield—was approximately accurate when coupon yields were in the 5 percent to 6 percent range and average mortgage life in the twelve- to twenty-year range (from Table 5, each two discount points charged on a 6 percent mortgage repaid in twelve years resulted in a 27 basis point increase in yield). But with current mortgage rates in the 9 percent range and average mortgage life closer to eight years, each two discount points raises the average effective yield by 39 basis points. This suggests that if lenders still use this rule of thumb to adjust effective yields, they are, on average, overadjusting by 50 percent.[4]

James R. Ostas has recently estimated the impact of state usury ceilings from a pooled cross section of quarterly observations on fifteen large Standard Metropolitan Statistical Areas (SMSAs).[5] His estimates provide support for the above contentions. Ostas found evidence that lenders close the gap between the ceiling and the competitive market rate by reducing the risk premium through higher downpayments and shorter maturities and by charging higher loan origination fees or more front-end points. Moreover, the effect of a 100 basis point difference between the "market" rate and the ceiling rate on loans is a 14½ percent decline in housing construction. The average difference in rates for the SMSAs in his data base during the period from 1965 through 1970 was 78 basis points, implying a reduction in construction of about 11½ percent during the observation period.[6]

This analysis implies that usury ceilings are especially detrimental to lower-income households with little wealth. Regrettably,

---

[4] Two articles in the *Federal Home Loan Bank Board Journal*, the first by Jerry Barrentine, "Estimating the Yield on Your Mortgage Investment," July 1974, and the second by Maurice Kinkade, "Mortgage Prepayments and Their Effects on S&L's," January 1976, found empirical evidence that the rule of thumb had, in fact, raised effective borrowing costs.

[5] James R. Ostas, "Effects of Usury Ceilings in the Mortgage Market," *The Journal of Finance*, June 1976, pp. 821–34.

[6] Another recent study—Philip K. Robins, "The Effects of State Usury Ceilings on Single Family Homebuilding," *Journal of Finance*, March 1974, pp. 227–35—concludes that a 100 basis point increase in usury ceilings during periods when they were below market rates would generate a 16 percent increase in single family housing starts.

those households which stand to benefit from the ceilings are more affluent and politically active. Therefore, it would presumably be very difficult to obtain the necessary political support to rescind the ceilings. Moreover, there is little that can be accomplished on a national level because usury ceilings are established by individual state governments. A plan for a federal override of state ceilings was recently considered, but such action does not appear to be constitutional. It would apparently be very difficult to legislate a state-by-state increase in the ceiling sufficient to ensure that the ceilings would not be binding in the next boom. Opponents of this move would probably argue that the ceiling "sets" mortgage rates in local markets, and that a large increase in the ceiling would exclude low-income families from homeownership. A third policy option, which some states have chosen, is to push for a flexible ceiling pegged sufficiently above a suitable market rate to prevent it from becoming effective.

FHA/VA Interest Rate Ceilings

A ceiling on the coupon rate on FHA/VA mortgages has been a feature of FHA/VA underwriting since the initiation of the programs. The intention of this feature was to prevent overcharging borrowers who were unfamiliar with mortgage finance and contemporaneous mortgage rates. As usual, this feature was designed to benefit lower-income borrowers who are viewed as being susceptible to "unscrupulous" lenders. In this regard, the rationale for an FHA/VA ceiling does not differ from that for state usury ceilings.

Changes in the ceiling were initially envisioned in response to changes in mortgage market conditions and market interest rates. Home mortgage rates were remarkably stable from the mid-1950s until the mid-1960s, so few changes in the ceiling rate were necessary. The ceiling does not appear to have been below market rates prior to the middle 1960s. In recent years, however, mortgage rates have been much more volatile, necessitating closer attention to market developments and more frequent changes in the ceiling rate. Unfortunately, changes in the ceiling rate have taken on significant political overtones. The "announcement effects" are somewhat comparable to those created by changes in the discount rate by the Federal Reserve Board. The announcement of a change in the discount rate is read by many as a shift in monetary policy. Because borrowers and lenders may respond to the perceived policy shift in undesirable ways, policy makers have sometimes been reluctant to change the rate when market conditions warranted it. Similarly, changes in the FHA ceiling rate have become indicators of shifts in the administration's housing policy. As a result, the secretary of HUD has often been reluctant to raise the FHA ceiling rate when market rates rose.

The analogy between the FHA ceiling rate and the Federal Reserve discount rate is worth pursuing because it highlights some misconceptions about the importance of the former. The Federal Reserve is sometimes viewed as determining short-term market rates via changes in the discount rate. A more appropriate view might be that the Federal Reserve determines short-term market rates by supplying the necessary amount of funds via open-market operations and then adjusts the discount rate accordingly. In either case, a strong correlation between changes in the administered discount rate and short-term market rates is observed, and one could argue that the process in which the discount rate is set determines short-term rates. Similarly, movements in the FHA ceiling rate are often said to cause movements in the market mortgage rate. This notion is essentially frivolous because the key policy tool, control over the total supply of funds, is missing.

The principal impact of lowering the FHA/VA ceiling rate relative to market-determined rates is the same as that of below-market usury ceilings—an increase in effective downpayment ratios. This is achieved by lenders charging points. This practice may discriminate even more against the lower-income mortgagee when applied to FHA/VA mortgages than when applied to conventionals because FHA typically insures mortgages of less affluent borrowers. Further, as noted above, the more quickly a loan with given points is repaid, the greater is the return to the lender. Thus, the lender has an incentive to foreclose or assign the loan to FHA at par when default occurs, recapture the principal, and keep the points.[7]

This should not be interpreted as conclusive evidence that the ceiling does not at times limit the availability of FHA mortgage credit. If FHA/VA and conventional mortgages were perfect substitutes, all lenders would shift to the unconstrained conventional market and avoid the ceiling, or lenders would charge sufficient points to raise the effective yield to the going market rate. This has not occurred because mortgage bankers and others who originate mortgage loans

---

[7] FHA loan originators must meet certain forbearance requirements before foreclosing on a mortgage in default of payments. After meeting these requirements, the originator may either foreclose, or, if certain conditions are met, assign the mortgage to FHA. Sources in FHA have attributed some cases of sloppy underwriting in the past to this incentive.

for investment by clients prefer the greater liquidity of FHA mortgages. They may, in fact, temporarily be willing to accept small capital losses on the sale of mortgages when the ceiling is binding in order to receive the future income from servicing the mortgages. However, the sensitivity of discretionary investors to binding FHA/VA ceilings appears to have increased substantially in the 1970s. From 1967 through 1971, FHA-insured loans accounted for 5 percent of the net change in holdings of home mortgages by commercial banks, mutual savings banks, and life insurance companies. From 1971 through 1975, this share fell to minus 22 percent as existing stocks of FHA mortgages matured.

It has been suggested that the reason for the decline in FHA/VA activity may be related to FHA underwriting requirements and processing.[8] Lenders making FHA/VA loans entail higher origination and servicing costs and face longer delays in application processing than they do when making conventional mortgages. These factors have always limited FHA/VA underwriting, however. Innovations in the mortgage market may provide a more plausible reason for lender reluctance to handle FHA/VA loans. First, the continued growth of private mortgage insurance has eliminated the FHA/VA underwriting monopoly. Second, conventional mortgages are now traded extensively by the FHLMC and FNMA, vastly improving their marketability for mortgage bankers. In addition, private trading of conventional mortgages has been somewhat facilitated by the FHLB's implementation of a nationwide automated network which provides detailed information on secondary mortgage market offerings. Moreover, the FHLMC issues pass-through securities on pools of conventional mortgages; the volume in 1977 reached almost $5 billion. Further, the FHLMC, as well as individual thrift institutions, can issue mortgage-backed bonds on pools of conventional mortgages. Few have been issued, however, because of the decline in mortgage rates relative to bond yields,[9] and it has been proposed by GNMA that it be given authority to issue pass-through securities on pools of conventionals. The continued growth and prosperity of these new markets and instruments and, in particular, the introduction of a GNMA conventional pass-through will make it increasingly difficult to attract lenders to FHA mortgages at below-market yields.

---

[8] *The Future Role of FHA*, Report of the FHA Task Force, July 1976.

[9] In 1977 a number of issues were placed. The phenomenal demand for mortgage credit in late 1976 and 1977 (and modest corporate bond issues) raised mortgage rates relative to bond rates, making issues of mortgage-backed bonds feasible.

Summary

Lenders respond in two ways to usury laws that prevent the quoted yields on home mortgage loans from rising to market-determined levels. They opt for less risky loans, and they charge points on riskier loans in an attempt to raise the effective yield to the market-determined level. The first is achieved by an increase in the down-payment ratio, and the second is equivalent to an increase in the ratio. Higher downpayment ratios are particularly burdensome to less wealthy households, those that usury laws purport to benefit. To the extent that there is a reduced demand for mortgage credit at the higher downpayment ratios or that lenders are prevented from obtaining risk-adjusted rates of return equal to those available in other credit markets, lenders will shift their funds to these other markets, particularly those for corporate bonds and commercial mortgages.

Proponents of usury ceilings argue that there is a gainer for every loser and thus that some borrowers will benefit by paying less for mortgage credit than appears warranted by the risk characteristics of their mortgage loan. The gainers are, however, likely to be the wealthier, less risky households and businesses. Both of these groups will benefit when discretionary lenders shift their funds to other credit markets, lowering the yields on corporate bonds, commercial mortgages, and business loans relative to what they would otherwise be. The usury ceilings effectively "crowd out" riskier household borrowers. While a few riskier households might in fact obtain cheaper credit, it is unlikely that this gain outweighs the loss of those riskier households that are shut out of credit markets.

Just as usury laws do not determine market mortgage rates, the secretary of HUD does not "set" mortgage rates by altering FHA/VA ceilings. If the ceiling is below the market rate, then lenders charge points to raise the effective rate. This raises effective downpayments and discriminates against short-term buyers. The increase in effective downpayments on FHA/VA mortgages is particularly disturbing because FHA studies indicate that they typically insure mortgages of less affluent families who are least able to make higher downpayments. In summary, binding FHA/VA ceilings can only harm those households they are supposed to protect.

5

Deposit Rate Ceilings at Financial Intermediaries

The rapid rise in interest rates on short-term open-market securities in 1966 posed a significant problem for commercial banks because these securities compete directly in asset portfolios with the large negotiable certificates of deposits (CDs) of banks. The Federal Reserve Board feared that banks would not be able to roll over their large stock of CDs outstanding at the ceiling rate. A large drop in bank deposits could have precipitated a scramble for liquidity from other sources, generating the widespread sale of Treasury securities or increased borrowing at the discount window. To avoid a bank liquidity problem and the disruption this might have created in the financial markets, Regulation Q ceilings on CDs were raised by 100 basis points in December 1965 to 5½ percent. Ceiling rates on other bank accounts were increased to the same level.

Large commercial banks rapidly took advantage of the increased ceilings to bid aggressively for deposits. This created two problems. First, smaller commercial banks, fearing reduced profits, lobbied intensively against the higher deposit rates. Second, the higher bank deposit rates generated a flow of funds from thrifts to banks. In the summer of 1966 the flow was substantial and the net increase in deposits at savings and loans during the entire year was less than any other year since 1953.

The consequences of this decline for the mortgage and housing markets have been well documented. By July 1966, tight mortgage credit had induced a 40 percent drop in housing starts, and it became clear to policy makers that thrifts could not compete effectively with commercial banks under these tight money market conditions. Because the asset portfolios of thrifts are relatively long term, the impact of a general rise in interest rates on thrift interest income develops only gradually as existing assets mature and are replaced by new, higher-yielding investments. Commercial banks, with much shorter-term asset portfolios, experience the benefits of higher yields more rapidly and thus can better afford to raise deposit rates.

In response to the pressures from smaller commercial banks, thrifts, and other parts of the housing lobby, the Interest Rate Adjustment Act of 1966 was passed. Under it deposit rate ceilings were extended for the first time to thrift accounts, and the ceilings on bank time deposits, other than CDs, were rolled back to 5 percent. From 1966 until 1970 thrifts were allowed to pay 75 basis points more than banks on regular passbook acounts and 25 basis points more on longer-term, less liquid accounts. The level of the ceilings was also unchanged until 1970.

The imposition of binding deposit rate ceilings represented an attempt to protect thrifts, and the mortgage and housing markets, from bank competition until market interest rates returned to normal levels. Unfortunately, interest rates never did. After a slight decline in early 1967 they rose to much higher peaks in early 1970 and even higher levels in 1974. As a result, the ceilings have been effective almost continuously since 1966.

The reasonableness of the use of deposit ceilings as a device to protect housing finance has been questioned because the impact of the ceilings on thrifts and the mortgage markets is ambiguous.[1] Theoretically, the direction and magnitude of the impact depend on relative interest rate responses in the demands and supplies for financial instruments. This argument is developed in the next section. Competition within the savings-account market and substitution between savings accounts and open-market securities during the last twenty-five years are then examined. An assessment of the past and the likely future impact of ceilings is presented in a concluding section.

Theoretical Underpinnings for Deposit Rate Ceilings

Although deposit rate ceilings have become a permanent feature of our financial system, there is no general agreement on their ultimate impact. Organized labor, for example, has consistently argued that

---

[1] See, for example, Paul Samuelson, "An Analytical Evaluation of Interest Rate Ceilings for Savings and Loan Associations and Competitive Institutions," Irwin Friend, ed., *Study of the Savings and Loan Industry* (Washington, D.C.: Federal Home Loan Bank Board, 1969).

ceilings lower the cost of mortgage credit by lowering the cost of funds to mortgage-lending deposit intermediaries. A number of economists, on the other hand, have constructed models in which thrift deposits decline when ceilings push deposit rates down, restricting the flow of mortgage credit and raising mortgage rates.[2] A similar model of the deposit and mortgage markets underlies both views but different assumptions regarding the competitiveness of the deposit market lead to different conclusions.

In a highly competitive financial system, the deposit rate at financial intermediaries will be linked closely with the rates in other financial markets. The general level of interest rates will be determined by the aggregate supply of and demand for loanable funds. The difference between after-tax rates will reflect only the inherent differences in the various institutional arrangements for borrowing and lending—administrative costs, risk, maturity, liquidity, et cetera—and the value placed on these characteristics by investors. Attempts to lower the interest rate in one deposit market through rate controls are fruitless because lenders would quickly move their funds to other markets and borrowers would follow. The regulated deposit market would dry up, and the rate differentials and relative credit flows in the remaining markets would remain unchanged. Similarly, attempts to lower rates in all deposit markets via rate controls are ineffective when deposits and open-market securities are close substitutes.

Suppose, in contrast, that markets are not highly competitive and that a binding ceiling is imposed on the rate commercial banks can pay on their deposits. If the bank deposit market is largely segmented from both the thrift deposit market and the securities market, then an increase in market interest rates (including those on bank loans) will not cause commercial banks to lose a significant amount of deposits to thrifts and the open market. Moreover, the ceiling prevents competition between banks, resulting in constant deposit costs. The increase in the bank loan rate raises profits. Increased long-run profitability should result in the formation of new banks and, especially, the establishment of new branches for existing banks. In other words, commercial banks will compete for deposits via nonprice mechanisms when ceilings prevent price competition. If potential new markets for savings exist, the ceilings could induce an expansion of deposits over the long run both by raising the share of savings going

---

[2] For a discussion of the position and views of labor, academics and others, see Donald Hester, "Special Interests: The FINE Situation," *Journal of Money, Credit, and Banking*, November 1977, pp. 652–61.

to commercial banks and by generating new savings that previously did not take place for lack of a desirable financial vehicle.

The impact of deposit rate ceilings on the mortgage rate depends on the structure of that market, as well as the deposit market. If the mortgage market is perfectly competitive, then credit will flow into and out of the market to neutralize rate changes induced by changes in deposit flows. That is, increased purchases by thrifts would be off-set by decreased purchases of others, leaving relative interest rates and total mortgage credit unchanged. But if the mortgage market is significantly segmented from other long-term securities markets, then deposit rates and flows will influence the mortgage rate and flows. The residential mortgage market does seem to be somewhat segmented because of the regulatory constraints on portfolio investments and tax incentives given to thrifts (particularly SLAs) to invest in residential mortgages. Thus, change in deposit flows to thrifts, to the extent that they are not offset by changes in advances (loans) from the FHLBS, will have some impact on the mortgage market.

Regulation Q and Competition between Banks and Thrifts

Ceilings on the allowable rate of interest on deposits at financial institutions have been a feature of our financial system since the Banking Act of 1933. At that time the Federal Reserve Board viewed the newly instituted Regulation Q (which limited the rate commercial banks could pay on time deposits and forbade interest on demand deposits) as a cure for the high rate of bank failures. Senator Glass, a sponsor of the Banking Act of 1933, said the provision was intended to "put a stop to the competition between banks in payment of interest which frequently induces banks to pay excessive interest on time deposits and has many times over again brought banks into serious trouble."[3] Actually, empirical research has indicated that the commercial banks offering the highest rates were also the soundest banks financially.[4] The deposit rate ceilings thus served to protect the weaker, less efficient banks from the competition of their stronger rivals.

Although some commercial banks offered the ceiling rate on deposits during the 1930s and 1940s, the average rate paid on deposits

---

[3] U.S. Congress, Senate, Committee on Banking and Currency, *Hearings on the Banking Act of 1933*, April 1933.

[4] Albert Cox, Jr., "Regulation of Interest Rates on Bank Deposits," Bureau of Business Research, University of Michigan, 1966.

was well below the ceiling. The average bank time-deposit rate bottomed out at 0.8 percent in 1946, and then began its gradual but persistent post-World War II rise. The ceiling rate does not appear to have limited commercial bank competition for deposits between 1933 and the early 1950s.

By 1956, the average rate paid on time deposits reached its previous 1936 peak and was still rising. More banks were paying the ceiling rate than at any previous time. It became evident to the Federal Reserve that the ceiling was limiting normal competition (as opposed to "ruinous" competition) by some banks. On the first day of 1957, the ceiling was raised by as much as 50 basis points on longer-term deposits. Regulation Q ceilings were raised again in 1961, 1962, 1963, and 1964, as average time and savings deposit rates approached the ceiling. In fact, until the credit crunch of 1966, the Federal Reserve Board raised the ceilings each time they became significantly binding. Nonetheless, there are several indications that commercial banks were more limited by Regulation Q ceilings during the first half of the 1960s than they had been in the past. First, the average rate paid on deposits by commercial banks was closer to the ceiling rate, and more of the larger city banks paid the ceiling rate during this period than in the past. Second, many larger banks utilized a newly created liability instrument, the large negotiable certificate of deposit (CD) to attract funds. (Interest rates on CDs were not regulated until 1966.)

Changes in competition for funds by depository institutions during the 1950s and early 1960s generated marked shifts in the distribution of household savings accounts among depository institutions. The shares of the growth in household time and savings accounts (excluding large CDs) that each of the depository institutions obtained during five-year intervals between 1950 and 1975 are listed in Table 6. During the 1950s, SLAs grew at a phenomenal pace, doubling total assets about every five years and attracting almost half of household savings deposits. This was a large increase over the one-fifth market share with which they began the decade. Issuing deposits and purchasing mortgages was an extremely profitable business because of a large spread between the mortgage and deposit rates. Thrifts attracted funds both by branching and by offering higher yields. Commercial banks were reluctant to raise yields, fearing a shift of interest-free demand deposits to interest-bearing time and savings accounts.

By the late 1950s and early 1960s, banks had had enough. They had seen their share of the time and savings-account market decline

TABLE 6

The Shares of the Net Increases in Household Deposits (Excluding cds) Attracted by the Depository Institutions

Depository institutions	1951–55	1956–60	1961–65	1966–70	1971–75
Commercial banks	29	31	43	52	44
Savings and loans	46	51	40	28	40
Mutual savings banks	21	14	13	15	11
Credit unions	4	4	4	5	5

Source: *Federal Reserve Flow of Funds Accounts.* cds are large (over $100,000) negotiable deposits at weekly reporting banks. Estimates of household holdings of cds constructed by the authors.

from 48 percent to 38 percent during the 1950s, and now their demand deposits were shifting to time accounts—and at thrifts at that. The commercial banks' share of the increase in household savings accounts jumped from 31 percent in the second half of the 1950s to 43 percent in the first half of the 1960s and to 52 percent in the second half. The sla share dropped from 51 percent to 40 percent and then to 28 percent. (The shares of mutual savings banks and credit unions were virtually unchanged.) Not surprisingly, the slower growth in funds and higher deposit rates had a negative impact on sla earnings and capital. The rate of growth in sla retained earnings averaged nearly 15 percent from 1950 through 1962. It then dropped to about 10 percent during the 1963–1965 period and to 7 percent for the 1966–1970 span.

Since 1966 thrifts have been allowed to pay a maximum differential, currently 25 basis points, more than commercial banks. The differential has been established to maintain parity between banks and thrifts because banks' monopoly on checking accounts (and consumer credit powers) give them an inherent advantage in competition for savings accounts. Because of the rate ceilings, competition between the institutions in the form of advertising, branching, and a wide variety of financial services has intensified. One by-product of the branching may have been the elimination of many local deposit market monopolies. Data for the 1971–1975 period indicate that thrifts have been successful in regaining the same share of the new savings account market that they had during the 1961–1965 period.[5]

Competition between Savings Accounts and Open-Market Securities

The regulators and thrifts had another lesson to learn: commercial bank deposits are not the only substitutes for thrift accounts in household portfolios. By the late 1960s the combination of continually rising yields on open-market securities and the unchanged deposit rate ceilings had made all savings deposits unattractive to investors with sufficient resources to purchase market securities. Disintermediation, the channeling of an unusually large proportion of household net purchases of discretionary assets (savings deposits plus credit market instruments) to credit market instruments, was hardly a new phenomenon. In 1955, and again in 1959 when the Treasury offered a 5 percent yield on five-year notes, flows to depository institutions fell off sharply. What was unusual about 1969 was the extent of the falloff and the small portion of the depository share that went to SLAS. Data on disintermediation and its effect on the resources of SLAS are given in Table 7. Four ratios are provided for the years 1955, 1959, 1966, 1969, and 1974, in which interest rates were at cyclically high levels.

The first ratio is the share of household net purchases of discretionary assets (savings accounts plus credit market instruments or open-market securities) going to depository institutions. In years of intermediation, such as 1967, 1971–1972, and 1975–1976, 90 percent and more of these funds are intermediated. As can be seen, in the 1950s just over 50 percent of the funds went to savings institutions even in the worst years, and 56 percent did so in the so-called crunch year of 1966. But in 1969 only a third went to depository institutions. This was truly the "crunch" year.

The second ratio in Table 7 is the percentage of the increase in deposits captured by SLAS. As was noted earlier, SLAS did very well in the 1950s and were hard hit in 1966 before the ceiling rates at banks were lowered. Not surprisingly, SLAS did relatively better in 1969.

---

[5] For a period in 1973 deposit rate ceilings were removed on four-year certificates with denominations of $1,000 or more. For an enlightened discussion of this episode, see Edward J. Kane, "Getting Along without Regulation Q: Testing the Standard View of Deposit Rate Competition during the 'Wild-Card Experience'," *Journal of Finance*, June 1978.

TABLE 7

The Share of Increments in Household Funds Going to Savings and Loan Associations in Years of Disintermediation

	(1) $\dfrac{\Delta SV}{\Delta SV + \Delta CMI}$	(2) $\dfrac{\Delta SVSL}{\Delta SV}$	$(1) \times (2)$ $\dfrac{\Delta SVSL}{\Delta SV + \Delta CMI}$	$\dfrac{\Delta SVSL + \Delta ADV}{\Delta SV + \Delta CMI}$
1955	.52	.56	.29	.33
1959	.51	.59	.30	.35
1966	.56	.20	.11	.16
1969	.33	.30	.10	.19
1974	.47	.36	.17	.23

SV = household savings deposits (excluding CDs) at all depository institutions.
CMI = household credit market instruments (including CDs).
SVSL = household savings deposits at SLAS.
ADV = advances (loans) from FHLBS to SLAS, less SLA equity in FHLBS.
SOURCE: *Federal Reserve Flow of Funds Accounts.*

(It is of historical interest that funds were shifted more heavily from commercial banks than from SLAS during bouts of disintermediation in the 1950s; this is no longer the case.) The third column is the share of total funds going to SLAS and is calculated as the product of the first and second columns. As can be seen, SLAS fared equally badly in 1966 and 1969, when they received only one-tenth of household funds (one-third of the fraction in the 1950s). The final column adjusts the SLA share to account for net lending from the FHLBS to offset the reduced share of household funds flowing directly to SLAS. Advances have supplemented SLA funds in all disintermediation years. The increase in the ratio of effective SLA funds to total funds was about 5 percent in 1955, 1959, and 1966 and nearly double that in 1969.

The substantial disintermediation in 1969 triggered two responses. First, deposit rate ceilings were raised by 25 to 75 basis points in early 1970 to permit a more normal relationship between yields in depository and open-market securities. Second, savings institutions attempted to lengthen the maturity of their deposits to reduce the sensitivity of the accounts to temporarily high open-market rates. Data in Table 8 suggest that SLAS have been quite successful in this regard. Passbook accounts actually fell between mid-1965 and the end of 1968, while certificates blossomed. Passbooks continued to decline into 1971 and then rose slowly, reaching their mid-1965

TABLE 8

PASSBOOK AND SPECIAL ACCOUNTS AT SAVINGS AND LOAN
ASSOCIATIONS
(billions of dollars)

Account	mid-1965	end 1968	mid-1971	end 1974	end 1976
Passbook	104	95	91	105	135
Certificates and special accounts	2	37	71	138	202

SOURCE: Savings and Loan *Fact Book.*

level by the end of 1974. Certificates and special accounts, in contrast, doubled between the end of 1968 and mid-1971 and again by the end of 1974 for a cumulative gain of $101 billion. By the end of 1976 certificates were 50 percent greater than passbook accounts. The recent growth in certificates has been assisted by the introduction of a two-year certificate in early 1970 followed by four- and six-year accounts in 1973 and 1974. (An eight-year account became available in 1978.)

Returning to the data in Table 7, we see that depository institutions in general, and SLAs in particular, fared significantly better during the 1974 period of disintermediation than in 1969. The share of funds going to depository institutions was up from 33 percent to 47 percent, and SLAs took 36 percent of this, reflecting their general improvement vis-à-vis commercial banks in the 1970s (see Table 6). Nonetheless, even with a further increase in deposit rate ceilings in 1973 and a substantial lengthening of the maturity of savings deposits, disintermediation was greater than in the 1950s and 1966.

Each episode of binding deposit ceilings has renewed interest in ways to avoid them. During the most recent episode, several new instruments were developed with the specific intent of attracting the funds of small depositors. The most important was the money market investment companies that issue money market mutual fund shares. From a base of only $200 million combined total assets in early 1974, these funds grew to about $3.7 billion by the end of 1975.

There are several types of money market funds. The most popular type, commonly called money market mutual funds, is directly analogous to common stock open-end investment companies. Most of these funds have attempted to duplicate the convenience and liquidity of passbook savings accounts while offering market yields.

Some have established checking account arrangements that allow customers to write checks on the shares and receive interest until the check clears the bank. These funds have essentially established interest-bearing checking accounts, and this interest can be substantial. In mid-1974, the average yield on money market funds was over 11 percent, more than double the passbook ceiling rate.

The second type of fund is a unit investment fund (analogous to a closed-end investment company). The sole purpose of this type of fund is to avoid the minimum purchase requirements of large denomination certificates of deposits. These requirements are intended to prevent the small depositor from switching to CDs when rates rise. The unit investment trust is an organization of individual investors who pool their funds to buy large denomination CDs. The pool is terminated when the CD expires, but individual investors may get out before termination by selling their shares on the secondary market or redeeming their shares at net asset value with the trustee. Consequently, unit investment trusts provide CD market yields and passbook liquidity. Although the funds appeal to a variety of investors, the bulk of shares are purchased by individuals with savings that would otherwise be in time and savings accounts at commercial banks and thrift institutions. At the end of 1975, $2.1 billion of the total $3.7 billion was invested in commercial bank CDs. Consequently, the funds represent a way for commercial banks to avoid deposit rate ceilings by paying market rates for deposits when interest rates rise, thus maintaining or increasing total deposits. These instruments ultimately divert the flow of funds from mortgage lending thrifts to the markets in which commercial banks specialize: Treasury securities, business loans, and consumer credit.

Another innovation in the financial markets motivated by binding interest rate ceilings is the variable-rate notes issued by commercial bank holding companies. These notes substituted primarily for commercial paper financing of nonbank subsidiaries, but they also represent a different source of funds. Whereas the average institutional order for commercial paper is about $500,000, the average size of the order for the variable rate notes was about $10,000. This suggests that small investors, those who typically invest in time and savings deposits, are the primary buyers of variable-rate notes. This attractiveness is explained by the market yield—floating note rates have been set at the Treasury bill rate plus 1 percent. There have been only three times in the last decade when this yield was below the maximum available on deposits, so it is unlikely that thrifts could compete with these securities even during slack periods. One bank added the proviso that it could pay more than 1 percent above the Treasury yield, virtually eliminating all possibility for competition from deposits.

In June 1977, an investment firm offered the first GNMA open-end mutual fund. The irony of this development is that the GNMA security was devised to attract new *institutional* funds to the mortgage market, whereas the mutual fund concept was devised to leap-frog deposit rate ceilings and attract the funds of *small* investors. The development of a GNMA mutual fund is illustrative of the adjustments the financial system is capable of making to avoid controls. Ultimately, the constrained institutions (thrifts) are replaced by unconstrained institutions (mutual funds) to restore the initial distribution of funds (household investment in mortgages).

Conclusion

Commercial banks were reluctant to compete aggressively for short-term deposit funds during the 1950s. For the most part they had sufficient funds to meet the needs of their business customers. More importantly, they did not want to generate a shift of interest-free demand deposits into interest-bearing time and savings accounts. Thus, although Regulation Q ceilings existed for commercial bank deposits, the ceilings were not binding.

In response to a decline in the share of savings accounts they attracted and a decline in the relative magnitude of demand deposits, banks competed more vigorously for savings accounts in the 1960s. Larger banks, which experienced particular difficulty in meeting loan demand, even turned to the open market by issuing large negotiable certificates of deposit. Bank deposit rates were raised until pressure from smaller commercial banks, thrifts, and the housing lobby generally led to a lowering of ceilings on bank deposits and an extension of ceilings to thrift accounts.

Thrift deposits and bank deposits have become much closer substitutes since 1965. In the absence of controls, rates at banks and thrifts would be about equal. Competition from open-market securities has also increased, in part because of the introduction of new instruments such as money market mutual funds. While this has increased the sensitivity of deposits to open-market yields, and thus the likely magnitude of disintermediation when market rates rise, the lengthening of the maturity of deposit accounts has reduced the sensitivity.

Deposit rate ceilings still serve their primary purpose, protection of thrift institutions, albeit not as effectively as in the past. The original need for protection—the inability of thrifts to compete with commercial banks over the rate cycle due to restrictions limiting them to long-term mortgages—still exists. Moreover, the relative decline in home mortgage yields generated by the activities of the federal credit agencies has put thrifts at even a long-run competitive disadvantage (or has reduced their previous advantage).

6

Costs and Benefits of the Current Financial Structure

The principal cost of the present financial system is the low or below-market interest rate received by depositors during periods of high open-market interest rates. Thrifts did not earn sufficient income during the 1968–1974 period to pay deposit rates competitive with open-market yields because thrifts invest heavily in long-term fixed-rate mortgages. Their mortgage portfolios earned relatively low income both because mortgage yields were lowered by the substantial purchases of the sponsored credit agencies and because thrift portfolios contained significant amounts of mortgages made at the lower yields existing prior to 1968. Homeowners with below-market fixed-rate mortgage financing benefited, but others who lost included those precluded from homeownership by higher downpayment requirements caused by usury and FHA/VA rate ceilings and by disintermediation stemming from deposit rate ceilings.

Depositors at commercial banks, like those of thrifts, lost interest income because of low deposit rates, but the motivation in this case was to protect thrifts from bank competition for funds rather than a lack of bank interest income to pay high deposit rates. Because of the predominately short-term asset holdings of commercial banks, their interest income rose sharply with the rise in interest rates during the late 1960s and 1973 and 1974. The gainers from low bank deposit rates were commercial bank stock holders, and possibly the holders of large CDs (and close substitutes) in 1973 and 1974, to whom banks were willing to offer extraordinary returns to secure funds.

Although the low cost fixed-rate mortgages generated by the present system are advantageous for homeowners and homebuilders, other aspects of the present system have less favorable implications

67

for these groups. In particular, the periodic episodes of disintermediation and binding usury and FHA/VA rate ceilings generated by sharply rising interest rates have induced severe cycles in housing sales and construction. This has made homebuilding an extremely risky business. There are fewer entrepreneurs willing to take this risk, and those who do so require higher *average* profit levels and employ relatively little capital. The consequence is higher housing prices than would exist with competitive deposit and mortgage markets.

Losses to Depositors and Gains to Others

David H. Pyle has calculated that depository institutions would have paid $5 billion extra interest to existing depositors during the 1968–1970 period in the absence of interest rate ceilings.[1] The calculation is obtained in three steps. First, equations were estimated over data from the 1952–1967 period to determine to which interest rates each of the depository institutions adjusted their own deposit rate and how rapidly the adjustment occurred. Second, these equations were used to deduce what rates each of the institutions would have paid during the 1968–1970 period in the absence of deposit rate ceilings. Third, the stock of deposits at each type of institution was multiplied by the difference between the rate the institutions would have paid and the rate actually paid. The sum of these products for the three institutions yields the $5 billion figure.

It seems likely to us that the $5 billion estimate is much too low. As noted in the last chapter, deposit markets probably became much more competitive during the late 1950s and early 1960s. Commercial banks and thrifts branched extensively into virtually all local markets, eliminating many local monopolies. Competition for short-term funds from the open market also became more intense, as evidenced by the development of money market mutual funds and variable-rate notes. This suggests that both commercial banks and thrifts would have raised their savings-account rates much more rapidly in response to the rise in interest rates in the late 1960s than predicted by Pyle's estimated equations, which were based on behavior going back to the early 1950s.[2] After examining a number of alternative hypothetical rate-setting relationships, we conclude that an

---

[1] David H. Pyle, "The Losses on Savings Deposits from Interest Rate Regulation," *The Bell Journal of Economics and Management Sciences*, Autumn 1974, pp. 614–22.

[2] For example, Pyle's equation for savings and loan associations implies that the speed at which they raise their deposit rate in response to a rise in the yield on five-year government bonds is only 15 percent per year.

estimate of $12½ billion of lost interest income to depositors is more plausible.[3] Moreover, a like amount was probably lost during the 1973–1975 bout of high market interest rates, raising the total loss to $25 billion.

The next question is, who gained the $25 billion lost in interest? A significant part of the gain was received by the depositors themselves as institutions competed for deposits by providing better services (branching, money machines, et cetera) and gifts in lieu of interest. Lewis J. Spellman suggests that Texas savings and loans paid an implicit return of a fifth of a percentage point more on deposits during the 1969–1972 period and two-fifths of a percentage point during 1973 and 1974.[4] If the latter also holds for 1975 and the entire analysis is applicable to all thrifts and commercial banks, then about $10 billion of the $25 billion was paid out to depositors. It should be understood that $10 billion in services and gifts is not equivalent in value to $10 billion in interest income. The difference in value is a deadweight loss of regulation, that is, there are no gains to offset the losses. (Although it might be further noted that households are less likely to pay taxes on gift income than on interest income.)

Most of the remaining net loss to depositors should be considered as going to either homeowners or taxpayers generally. If the federally sponsored credit agencies had not lowered mortgage rates relative to other yields and if thrifts had been allowed to make variable-rate mortgage loans instead of fixed-rate loans, then thrift interest income would have risen *pari passu* with the general rise in interest rates.[5] Rate ceilings would not have been needed; depositors would have earned a market rate of return. Under this interpretation, homeowners would be the primary recipients of the thrifts' share of the remaining $15 billion of net interest saved, or about $6 billion. An alternative interpretation is that the Treasury would have had to bail

---

[3] The $12½ billion was the lowest estimate obtained in a series of calculations in which passbook rates were related to the average three-month bill rates during the previous two to four years and certificate rates were dependent upon the one-year and/or three-to-five year Treasury yields during the current and previous year or two.

[4] Lewis J. Spellman, "Nonrate Competition for Savings Deposits," Federal Home Loan Bank of San Francisco, January 1977.

[5] For an analysis of the impact of the activities of the agencies on the distribution of income, see Patric H. Hendershott and Kevin E. Villani, "The Impact of Federal Mortgage Lending Policies on the Distribution of Income," forthcoming in K. Boulding and T. Wilson, eds., *Redistributing Income Via the Financial System: The Grants Economics of Money and Credit* (New York: Praeger Publishing Company, 1978), or Patric H. Hendershott, *Understanding Capital Markets, Volume I: A Flow-of-Funds Financial Model* (Lexington, Mass.: Lexington Books, 1977), chap. 16.

out the thrifts in the absence of rate ceilings to prevent them from bankruptcy. In this case, taxpayers were the beneficiaries of the ceilings on rates paid by thrifts. Regarding the $9 billion ($15 billion less $6 billion) net loss to depositors at commercial banks, the beneficiaries were likely shareholders of commercial banks and investors in large CDs and short-term open-market paper who earned extraordinary returns as banks competed for these funds.

An even more interesting issue than identifying the broad groups that gained at the expense of depositors is the impact of these gains and the losses of depositors on the distribution of income. The first three lines of Table 9 contain estimates of the distribution of savings account and primary security holdings and mortgage debt outstanding among income quintiles. Not surprisingly, most financial claims are held and issued by the highest-income quintile. This group earned 42 percent of household income in 1971 and probably had an even higher proportion of household wealth. Also not surprising is the preference of the higher-income (wealth) households for primary securities. Finally, data on the proportion of federal taxes paid by households in different income quintiles are consistent with the usual assumption that the effective federal tax is progressive.

The data base from which this distribution of asset holdings and liabilities outstanding is drawn is a 1962 sample survey of households

TABLE 9

PERCENTAGE DISTRIBUTION OF HOUSEHOLD ASSET HOLDINGS, MORTGAGE DEBT, AND FEDERAL TAX PAYMENTS BY INCOME QUINTILES[a]

	Low	Lower-middle	Middle	Upper-middle	High
Savings accounts	.10	.12	.12	.17	.49
Primary securities	.04	.10	.08	.17	.61
Mortgage debt	.02	.06	.17	.27	.48
Federal taxes	.03	.10	.15	.20	.52

[a] The approximate divisions between the income quintiles for 1975 were, in thousands of 1975 dollars, 7, 11.5, 16, and 22 (U.S. Bureau of the Census, *Statistical Abstract of the United States*, Table 537, 1975).
SOURCES: Savings accounts, primary securities, and mortgage debt divisions are constructed from D. Projector and G. Weiss, *Survey of Financial Characteristics of Consumers*, Board of Governors of the Federal Reserve System, August 1966, Tables A10–A19, pp. 118–30. Division of federal taxes paid is from *Allocating Tax Burdens by Income Class*, Tax Foundation, Inc., New York, 1967, Table 4, p. 7.

and is obviously outdated. There is no strong evidence to suggest shifts in this distribution since 1962, however, so no obvious bias exists. Moreover, recent evidence suggests very little change in the distribution of *monetary* income across income classes since 1962, indicating that unless savings and spending habits have changed markedly, the current distribution is probably similar to the distribution that existed in 1962.[6]

The impact of the low deposit rates on the distribution of income is calculated in the following way. First, the gainers are identified and the difference between the line in Table 9 associated with the gainers and the savings-account line is computed. If the gainers were mortgagors, the top line in Table 10 would be the result; a dollar shift from depositors to mortgagors will benefit those with middle and upper-middle incomes (by five cents and ten cents, respectively) because these groups have relatively more mortgage debt than savings-account holdings. Second, the impact of a dollar shift is multiplied by the total loss to depositors to deduce the total income transfer. Thus the second row in Table 10 is the product of $6 billion, the estimated total transfer from thrift depositors to mortgagors, and the values in row 1. Finally, the impact on the distribution of income of the deposit rate ceilings at both commercial banks and thrifts is combined to provide an estimate of the total effect. Given that there is a gainer for every loser, all rows in Table 10 sum horizontally to zero.

Alternative 1 for thrift accounts in Table 10 has already been explained in large part. When mortgagors are assumed to be the gainers, the lowest quintile loses nearly $500 million, the second lowest over $350 million, the middle quintile gains $300 million, the second-from-highest gains $600 million, and the highest loses slightly. As noted, these income shifts are explained by the distribution of savings-account holdings and home mortgage debt outstanding. The low and lower-middle income groups have low mortgage debt relative to savings-account holdings. Low income and wealth households are unable to meet downpayment requirements, while low income, wealthier households, predominately retirees, tend to have paid off their mortgages. Moreover, low-income households find renting relatively cheaper; the after-tax mortgage rate, and thus the cost of homeownership, is inversely related to income. Those with very high income, on the other hand, tend to spend relatively less of their

---

[6] Edgar K. Browning, "How Much More Equality Can We Afford?" *The Public Interest*, Spring 1976, Table 2, p. 93. Browning shows that the distribution of total income changed markedly when in-kind transfers are taken into account.

TABLE 10

GAINS OR LOSSES INDUCED BY DEPOSIT RATE CEILINGS, BY INCOME QUINTILES

	Low	Lower-middle
Thrift accounts		
Alternative 1. Mortgagors gain		
Impact of a dollar loss to savings account holders and gain to mortgagors (in dollars)	−.08	−.06
Total income transfer assuming a $6 billion loss (in millions of dollars)	−480	−360
Alternative 2. Taxpayers gain		
Impact of a dollar loss to savings account holders and gain to taxpayers (in dollars)	−.07	−.02
Total income transfer assuming a $6 billion loss (in millions of dollars)	−420	−120
Commercial bank accounts		
Impact of a dollar loss to savings account holders and gain to primary security holders (in dollars)	−.06	−.02
Total income transfer assuming a $9 billion loss (in millions of dollars)	−540	−180
Combined impact of thrift (Alternative 1) and commercial bank accounts	−1020	−540
Combined impact of thrift (Alternative 2) and commercial bank accounts	−960	−300

SOURCE: Table 9.

income on housing and to borrow a smaller proportion of the housing outlay. With relatively low mortgage debt, these quintiles benefit relatively little from low mortgage rates. The middle and upper-middle income households with relatively large mortgage debt are the gainers.

Under Alternative 2 federal taxpayers are the beneficiaries in that they are not required to pay the cost of low mortgage rate policies

Middle	Upper-middle	High	Sum
.05	.10	−.01	0
300	600	−60	0
.03	.03	.03	0
180	180	180	0
−.04	—	.12	0
−360	—	1080	0
−60	600	1020	0
−180	180	1260	0

directly or indirectly by subsidizing thrifts. The low and lower-middle quintiles are still net losers. The lowest quintile loses slightly less— just over $400 million—under these assumptions because of their low federal tax liabilities, and the loss to the second lowest quintile is cut sharply to just over $100 million. The gains are spread evenly over the highest three quintiles—nearly $200 million for each—because the difference between their tax burden and their share of savings-account holdings is the same. Under either alternative it seems clear that low deposit rates at thrift institutions are sharply detrimental to those in the lowest two income quintiles, particularly those in the lowest.

Turning now to the impact of low deposit rates at commercial banks, the biggest (and only) gainers are those in the highest income quintile. This is because they are the only quintile that invests relatively more heavily in primary securities than in savings accounts. Assuming that depositors at commercial banks lose $9 billion in total, those in the highest quintile, who undoubtedly hold most commercial bank equity and large negotiable CDs, gain over a billion dollars. Those in the upper-middle quintile break even, while those in the lowest three quintiles lose from just under $200 million to over $500 million. Again, the loss falls heaviest on the lowest quintile.

The combined impact of deposit rate ceilings at both thrifts and commercial banks on the distribution of income is listed at the bottom of Table 10 for both alternatives regarding the gainers from ceilings at thrifts (either mortgagors or taxpayers). As can be seen, the sharpest shifts are a billion dollar loss by those in the lowest quintile and over a billion dollar gain by those in the highest. Those in the upper-middle quintile gain either a modest or large—$600 million—amount depending on whether the benefits of low thrift deposit rates accrue to taxpayers or mortgagors. Those in the middle quintile lose slightly, while those in the lower-middle suffer a $300 million to $500 million setback. In conclusion, it would appear difficult to design a financial system that would do more to skew the distribution of income than the present system of low deposit rate ceilings.

Costs and Benefits of Housing Cycles

Housing is generally considered to be the component of aggregate demand most sensitive to financial conditions, and housing cycles are believed to be induced by changes in financial conditions.[7] Deposit rate ceilings, in conjunction with usury and FHA/VA mortgage interest rate ceilings, contribute to housing cycles by magnifying the impact on housing demand of changes in the supplies and demands for credit in other markets. Because these cycles cause housing construction to be an especially risky business and the industry to be labor intensive,

---

[7] See, for example, Lyle E. Gramley, "Short-Term Cycles in Housing Production: An Overview of the Problems and Possible Solutions," *Ways to Moderate Fluctuations in Housing Construction*, Federal Reserve Staff Study, 1972, pp. 7–10.

construction costs and sales prices are higher than they would be with the less volatile production schedules that would exist in the absence of deposit rate ceilings. This is an unambiguous cost of ceilings. On the other hand, housing demand may act as an automatic stabilizer for aggregate demand over the business cycle, in which case the existence of rate ceilings could provide a benefit for the economy by accentuating housing cycles.

This section begins with a discussion of the causes of housing cycles. Their costs (higher housing costs and prices) and benefits (a more stable aggregate economy) are then considered. The most controversial part of the analysis is related to the potential stabilization benefit of the volatility of housing demand induced by the financial structure. In our view, the stabilization benefits of housing cycles and thus the increased volatility of housing demand created by deposit rate ceilings are less than they are generally perceived to be.

Causes of Housing Cycles. The first task is to consider whether housing cycles are generated internally or represent a response to changing financial conditions induced by cycles in other expenditures. This is necessary in order to determine whether or not greater sensitivity of housing to financial conditions stabilizes economic activity, since the question partially hinges on the cause of housing cycles. There are no a priori reasons for assuming a cycle has internal or external origins. Housing construction is subject to the same cycle-generating disturbances as are other forms of investment. For example, just as exogenous rising profit expectations of businessmen can induce investment booms in manufacturing, they can cause booms in housing. In addition, housing construction has been subject to another volatile influence—stop-and-go government subsidies. The housing subsidy programs in the early 1970s contributed significantly to the unprecedented surge in housing starts in the 1970–1972 period.[8] Moreover, overbuilding during this boom worsened the decline in starts during the ensuing bust. The magnitude of this cycle suggests that this source of instability should not be taken lightly.

Nonetheless, most housing cycles appear to originate in the nonhousing sectors and to be transmitted to housing via changes in credit terms and availability. Housing demand is said to be more sensitive to financial conditions than other components of aggregate demand because housing is a more durable asset. That is, because housing represents a longer flow of future services, a given rise in

---

[8] John Weicher, "The Affordability of New Homes," *Journal of the American Real Estate and Urban Economics Association*, volume 5, no. 2 (1977), p. 212.

interest rates will reduce the value of housing by more than the value of other goods, resulting in a greater decline in demand.

This argument is an inadequate explanation of the relatively greater volatility in housing cycles. A restrictive monetary policy will not increase interest rates by the same amount on debt of all maturities. A restrictive policy will generally raise the current short-term (one-year) rate and the one-year rates expected to exist in the next year or two. Conceptually, the present value of long-term assets may be calculated by using either these one-year rates or the equivalent long-term rates to discount future services. In the previous example, it is the present value of the services from the investment in only the first two or three years that declines. The relative change in the present value of investment goods whose life exceeds three years is the same, regardless of differences in durability. The durable-goods hypothesis explains a greater elasticity of demand for durable goods with respect to interest rates. However, it does not imply more sensitivity to temporary shifts in monetary policy or credit market demands of goods with lives greater than three years than those with lives of three years.

There are alternative, more plausible explanations of the relatively greater sensitivity of housing demand to credit terms. First, a rise in interest rates to a level that is high by historical standards may be viewed as temporary. Because existing housing is an extremely good substitute for new housing, many households may be able to postpone construction of new homes with little loss of utility. A large part of business plant and equipment investment, however, is for the introduction of new technologies, new plants in areas of expanding growth, and the like, and for these there are few, if any, substitutes. The same is true to a lesser extent for state and local government investment; schools, roads, parks, and other municipal capital goods are generally constructed where none previously existed, and these investments may be less easily postponed.

The second reason why housing demand may be more sensitive to changes in financial conditions relates to the substitution of new for existing housing and the repayment of the mortgage associated with the latter. Most new homes are purchased by current homeowners who sell their previous home in the process of upgrading their housing. This contrasts with new plants and schools which are generally added to existing facilities by firms and governmental units. When interest rates rise, the market value of a long-term fixed-rate nontransferable mortgage contract falls. The difference between the par value and market value of the mortgage is the discounted present value of the interest saving—the difference between the higher new issue rate and existing contract rate, times the outstanding debt—to the homeowner. But in order to realize this saving the homeowner must maintain his place of residence; he cannot take the mortgage with him if he purchases another home, and he must repay the existing mortgage at par value. Thus, increases in income that would normally expand the demand for housing, even in the face of higher new mortgage rates, tend not to do so when mortgage rates are above earlier levels.[9]

A third reason is that financial regulations may increase the amplitude of housing cycles induced by financial market disturbances. Some mortgage market regulations—deposit rate ceilings in particular —tend to restrict the supply of mortgage credit during periods of credit stringency. This would push mortgage rates higher than other rates were it not for other regulations, notably FHA/VA and state usury ceilings on mortgage rates, which limit this rise. This increases the use of points which leads to changes in effective downpayment ratios. Given that this ratio is an important constraint on homeownership, changes in it have likely been an important cause of past housing cycles.

A Cost of Housing Cycles: Higher Housing Prices. Variability in housing demand affects the efficiency of housing production adversely in two ways. First, variability increases average production costs over the cycle because the marginal cost of housing increases as output expands. Marginal costs increase because builders bid up the prices of labor (overtime) and building materials to expand production. More homes are built at the peak of the cycle when costs are higher, so the average cost per unit is greater than with a stable level of production. Second, unstable production also probably induces builders to adopt labor-intensive modes of production that are less efficient for producing the optimal level of output. This would occur either because the labor-intensive mode is less costly, on average, for producing the varying levels of output that are required over the cycle or because the riskiness of the unstable production makes the cost of attracting financial capital too high to allow selection of a high-technology capital-intensive mode of production.

The second point is illustrated in terms of Figure 4. The left panel contains hypothetical short-run average cost curves for both

---

[9] To the extent that the yield on variable-rate mortgages (VRMS), discussed in chapter 7, moves with current new issue mortgage rates, the widespread use of VRMS would remove this impediment to the expansion of housing demand.

FIGURE 4

IMPACT OF VARIABLE PRODUCTION SCHEDULES ON BUILDER COSTS
AND INVESTMENT

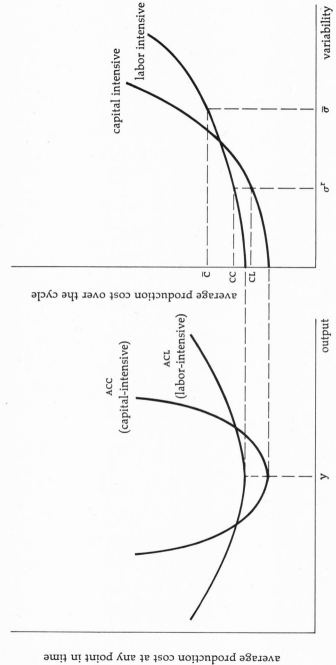

SOURCE: Authors' construction.

labor- and capital-intensive production functions. A capital-intensive mode of housing production, for example the prefabrication of houses in factories, will provide a lower average cost per unit over some narrow range of production levels. Average costs rise substantially more at lower production levels for the capital-intensive producer than the labor-intensive one because the former has higher fixed costs to average over fewer units. When production levels expand beyond the most efficient range, marginal costs probably rise rapidly for all producers. Given the substantial cyclical variability in housing demand generated by the present financial structure, it is not surprising that builders have selected a labor-intensive production process.[10]

A direct relationship between average costs over the building cycle and variable production is illustrated in the right panel of Figure 4. Average cost now represents the average of all units produced over the entire range of production levels chosen during a housing cycle. The average variability of output over the cycle is measured on the horizontal axis. Two average-cost over-the-cycle curves are drawn, based on the same quantity of capital and production processes underlying the short-run average cost curves in the left panel. If production did not vary at all over the cycle, then firms would continually operate at the output level, y. Thus the curves in the right panel touch the vertical axis at the respective minimum average cost points. As the variability of production increases, the average cost of units produced with a capital-intensive production process rises more rapidly than with a labor-intensive production process.

The average variability of housing production with the current housing finance system is denoted by σ. Given that firms have chosen the labor-intensive production process, the average cost (over the cycle) is $\overline{C}$. If financial reform reduces variability to σ^r, then average costs will fall for two reasons. First, even if builders continue to produce houses in the same labor-intensive manner, average costs will decline to CL. This results from producing closer to the minimum average cost. Second, builders will have an incentive to employ more capital, further reducing average costs to CC. The decline in average house prices resulting from this improvement could be substantial.

Highly variable production schedules have a similar impact on the costs of producing materials for housing construction. A less volatile

[10] William E. Gibson, "Protecting Home Building from Restrictive Credit Conditions," *Brookings Papers on Economic Activity*, vol. 3 (1973), pp. 675–82. Antiquated building codes and the reluctance of some unions to accept new production techniques contribute to the selection of the production process (Allan H. Meltzer, "Regulation Q: the Money Markets and Housing-I," *Housing and Monetary Policy*, FRB of Boston, Conference Series no. 4 [1970], pp. 41–51).

housing cycle would thus reduce materials costs (lower all four curves in Figure 4). Finally, homebuilders, material suppliers, and construction labor must all be compensated for the increased risk of investment and employment in the construction industry. The housing industry includes many small builders and suppliers who risk not only the current potential income from alternative, less risky employment, but also their personal wealth. Severe downturns in housing demand result in bankruptcy for a significant segment of the industry. This suggests that there are fewer firms engaged in the production of housing and building materials than there would be with more stable production patterns. Union and nonunion wages in the construction industry contain a premium for anticipated cyclical unemployment.

In conclusion, a more stable housing cycle would lower housing prices, and thus increase the demand for homeownership, by reducing factor prices, inducing a better (less expensive) factor mix, decreasing periods of inefficient (at levels other than minimum average cost) production, and lowering profit margins. Moreover, both construction labor and builders would be better off because of the reduced risk of receiving less than expected returns and the greater average level of production generated by lower housing prices.

The Stabilization Benefit of Housing Cycles. As noted above, a number of the features of the present financial system cause housing cycles to be more volatile than they would be in a less-regulated system.[11] These include restrictions against variable-rate mortgages (VRMs) and deposit, usury, and FHA/VA rate ceilings. The more volatile housing cycles that follow from these ceilings, and thus the regulations themselves, could be defended on the grounds that they contribute to the stabilization of aggregate economic activity.[12] Under some conditions, the greater sensitivity of housing demand to financial conditions will serve this purpose, but under circumstances that

---

[11] The restrictions, particularly deposit rate ceilings, might also aggravate housing by lengthening the downswing portion of the cycle relative to the upswing portion. The general level of interest rates appears to have risen by about 3 percentage points between the mid-1960s and mid-1970s, while deposit rate ceilings at thrifts have risen by only ½ (passbook accounts) to 2½ (six-year accounts) percentage points. Thus disintermediation might set in at an earlier stage of the interest rate cycle (the lengthening of the average maturity of thrift accounts acts to offset this tendency, while the development of smaller denomination open-market alternatives to thrift accounts, such as money market funds, reinforces the tendency).

[12] Arnold C. Harburger, "Discussion," *Housing and Monetary Policy*, FRB of Boston, Conference Series no. 4 (1970), p. 37.

may possibly be the most common, greater sensitivity may increase instability.

Whether or not greater stability ensues depends on the market in which the disturbance originates and the interest sensitivity of borrowers in this and other markets. Consider an "exogenous" increase in demand at full employment. There are several ways for the economy to respond to excess demand. If all borrowers, both those issuing securities to finance purchases of the goods in excess demand and those issuing securities to finance other investment, are quite insensitive with respect to interest rates, then interest rates will rise sharply. This will induce substantial economizing of money balances and thus financing of the excess demand (the velocity of money rises and inflation accelerates). If borrowers financing purchases of goods in excess demand are interest sensitive, then the rise in interest rates will directly choke off the excess demand with little resulting inflation. Lastly, if borrowers financing purchases of goods not in excess demand are relatively interest sensitive, then production of these goods will decline. In this manner, resources will be freed to increase production of the goods in excess demand and to offset the inflationary pressures in this manner.

This last case is most relevant to the U.S. economy. Corporations and the federal government are notoriously insensitive to interest rates, and disturbances typically originate in these sectors. Housing is very sensitive to financial conditions, particularly so because of the regulations mentioned above. Thus, resources are released from the production of houses when excess demand originates in the corporate or federal sector.

There are three necessary conditions for the release of these resources to reduce the inflationary pressure caused by the initial excess demand. First, housing construction must respond quickly to changes in financial conditions. Theoretically, an increase in interest rates causes a decline in the demand for the stock of housing and thus a fall in housing sales. The more rapidly housing starts decline in response to the buildup in the inventory of unsold units, the more rapidly resources are freed from the production of housing. The second requirement is that the resources employed in the construction of housing are also useful in the production of the good in excess demand. Single-family housing construction requires large amounts of relatively unskilled labor (about 15 percent of the total labor necessary for this construction activity) that is useful in the production of many other goods, particularly multifamily construction. The extent to which this labor is transferable depends on where the disturbance originated.[13] The final requirement is that resources be mobile. Factors of production must be able to move quickly from industries with excess supply to industries with excess demand. This requirement is the most difficult to meet in the case of labor. Even though residential construction workers are probably the most mobile members of the labor force, they may not be mobile enough to ensure stability.[14]

What happens if these three requirements are not met? First, most of the labor and material resources released from the production of housing remain unemployed. The decline in housing production thus results in a reduction in real output. The induced unemployment reduces aggregate demand, although by far less than the decline in output, because workers in depressed industries continue to spend, financing this spending with unemployment benefits and past savings. The reduction in demand will eventually have a negative impact on plant and equipment outlays through a reduction in the sales of the products produced with the plant and equipment. However, this impact will probably be felt too late to dampen the inflationary pressures generated by the initial disturbance. Moreover, some of the reduction in the demand for housing may be translated into increased demands for other goods, such as consumer durables, creating inflationary pressures in other markets. In any event, the economy could be more stable if housing were insulated from the exogenous excess demand in the other sector, rather than being especially sensitized to it by regulatory constraints. Only if the disturbance occurs in the housing sector will the special sensitivity introduced by regulations contribute to economic stability.

This analysis has more general implications regarding the use of discretionary monetary policy. For disturbances originating in housing, the best way to stabilize the economy is to reinforce the tendency of interest rates to rise, thereby nipping the disturbance in the bud and stabilizing housing and the economy. The same is true for disturbances originating in other markets where the resources employed are particularly close substitutes for those used in housing. On the other hand, if demand increases for a good produced with resources that are not utilized in the production of housing, a restrictive monetary policy has little to recommend it. The policy will create unem-

---

[13] See Craig Swan, "Labor and Material Requirements for Housing," *Brookings Papers on Economic Activity*, vol. 2 (1971), pp. 357–59.

[14] On the mobility of construction workers, see John T. Dunlop and Daniel Q. Mills, "Manpower in Construction: A Profile of the Industry and Projections to 1975," in the *Report of the President's Committee on Urban Housing: Technical Studies*, vol. 2 (1968), pp. 239–86a.

ployment in the housing-related sectors and do little to dampen inflationary pressures in the market initially experiencing excess demand. What is needed in this circumstance is a contractionary policy action that will impact directly on the market in which the disturbance originated. Such an action might be a decrease in the business investment tax credit. The Federal Reserve Board study concluded that a reduced credit would diminish business investment in boom periods, thereby stabilizing housing construction.[15]

Summary

Regulation and intervention in the current financial system alter the competitive market determination of interest rates and credit flows. Specifically, federal intervention in the mortgage market in combination with thrift portfolio restrictions reduces mortgage rates; deposit rate ceilings allow deposit intermediaries to pass their lost interest income on to depositors. In addition to the income transfers resulting from these policies, they limit the ability of mortgage lenders to compete for funds during periods of credit restraint and thus magnify housing cycles.

Our estimates indicate that depositors lost about $25 billion in monetary interest payments over the past decade, but that about $10 billion of this was returned in the form of gifts and services. About 60 percent of the remaining $15 billion accrued to predominantly wealthy commercial bank CD holders and shareholders, with the rest accruing to homeowners. Because the benefits accrue to families of generally higher income and greater wealth than the families bearing the costs, the result is a regressive net redistribution of income. Households in the lowest income quintile have lost around a billion dollars and the second lowest nearly half a billion. The highest income quintile, in contrast, has probably gained in excess of a billion dollars.

The consequences of housing cycles for the housing industry and the nation's economy were also discussed. Housing cycles raise the cost of housing in several ways. First, variable production schedules raise the average cost of the variable inputs—labor and construction materials—employed in housing construction. This results from competition for inputs when production is expanding and from the premiums built into the price of these inputs as compensation for variable demand. Second, builders employ less capital and lower technology production techniques than would be economically feasible

---

[15] See, for example, Gramley, "Short-Term Cycles in Housing Production," pp. 45–50.

with more stable production patterns. Thus, they fail to utilize the latest cost-savings techniques. The final result for consumers is higher housing prices.

The last issue raised was the potential stabilizing influence that variable housing production is said to exert on aggregate economic activity. Whether or not housing cycles exert a stabilizing influence depends on the nature of the sector where the disturbance originates and the response of the monetary authorities. Under the most common circumstances—relatively immobile resources in the short run and disturbances originating in the corporate or federal sector—an especially sensitized housing sector probably contributes to greater, rather than lesser, instability.

7

Improving the Short-Run Viability of Thrifts

After exploring in detail the costs and benefits of the existing financial structure, the most severe cost appears to be the regressive redistribution of income caused by deposit rate ceilings. Equity requires that removal or at least the raising of deposit rate ceilings be the starting point of reform of the housing finance system. Most of the other reform proposals are simply an attempt to ensure the survival of thrifts (and maintain housing construction) in the absence of rate ceilings.

The actions necessary to make thrifts viable take two forms. First, thrifts must be allowed to provide the same services to households that banks provide if the former are to be able to compete on equal grounds with the latter for household savings accounts. Second, thrifts must either balance the maturity of their asset and liability portfolios or have some means for neutralizing the possible cash flow and/or insolvency problems that imbalance might induce.[1] This chapter deals with proposals to extend thrift asset powers, to expand thrift liability authorities, and to stabilize thrift cash flow.

These changes are necessary, but not sufficient, to enable thrifts to pay the same deposit rate over the long run that commercial banks are able to pay. Thrifts have been at a disadvantage because of their heavy investment in low-yielding home mortgages. Possible solutions to the problem of being restricted to investing in home mortgages that earn a below free-market rate of return are discussed in the next chapter.

---

[1] For an excellent discussion of alternative means of solving the maturity imbalance problem, see Dwight M. Jaffee, "The Asset/Liability Maturity Mix of s&ls: Problems and Solutions," *Change in the Saving and Loan Industry*, Proceedings of the Second Annual Conference, FHLB of San Francisco, 1976, pp. 59–88.

Expanded Investment Powers

One obvious reform is to remove the portfolio restrictions underlying the relative specialization of thrifts in mortgages. Complete removal has never been seriously considered, however, for two reasons. First, any steps that appear likely to reduce the total supply of mortgage credit are an anathema to the housing interests. Second, thrifts have never expressed strong interest in investing in nonmortgage assets. Consequently, proposals for expanding the investment powers of thrifts typically contain only minor extensions into the areas of consumer credit and corporate debt. A very important element of reform, however, is the removal of strictures against investment in variable-rate mortgage loans.

Consumer Loans. The Financial Institutions Act of 1975 proposed a 10 percent limit on the percentage of assets SLAS and MSBS should be allowed to invest in consumer credit.[2] Other reform proposals have included similar provisions. While federally chartered SLAS currently do not have this authority, the service corporations and subsidiaries of multiple savings and loan holding companies were given the authority in April 1975 to make, buy, and sell consumer loans. And some state-chartered institutions currently have the authority.

How would extending this authority to all SLAS affect SLA investment and earnings? Thrifts seem unlikely to invest anywhere near 10 percent of their assets in consumer credit. Analysis of the net return on consumer loans shows it to be lower than is generally thought.[3] Further, the experience of MSBS in states where they already have the power to make consumer loans does not suggest substantial use of it. Only in one of ten states are consumer loans greater than 3½ percent of assets, and in most the percentage is in the 1 to 2 percent range.[4] The experience of state-chartered SLAS in Texas is similar. These institutions have only 2 to 2¼ percent of their portfolios in consumer credit.[5]

---

[2] Financial Institutions Act of 1975, U.S. Congress, Senate, Report of the Committee on Banking, Housing, and Urban Affairs, S. 1267, Washington, D.C., November 20, 1975.

[3] P. S. Anderson and R. W. Eisenmenger, "Structural Reform for Thrift Institutions: The Experience in the United States and Canada," *New England Economic Review*, July/August 1972, p. 10.

[4] Ibid., p. 10.

[5] Kenneth Thygerson, "The Case for Savings and Loan Participation in the Consumer Credit Market," mimeographed, August 1973.

Thrifts have two other motivations for wanting consumer credit authority. The first and less important is that it would marginally reduce the maturity of their asset portfolio. The second is that it would enhance the package of services they could offer households. This is one step in the direction of becoming "family financial centers," a development which they feel is necessary to meet the competition of "full service banks." For this second reason, consumer credit authority should be extended to thrifts. But granting consumer credit authority should not be viewed as a solution to the fundamental problems facing the thrift industry.

Corporate Debt. Some past reform proposals have included a provision to allow thrifts to invest some prespecified share of assets in high-grade corporate debt (the share was 10 percent in the Financial Institutions Act of 1975). Proponents argue that this will improve thrift earnings, thereby allowing them to compete more effectively with commercial banks. Opponents counter that it will reduce the supply of mortgage credit, and the result will be less housing.

The limited ability to invest in corporate bonds is not expected to have a large impact on thrift profits, particularly in the short run. Although bond yields are higher than mortgage rates after adjustment for differences in transaction costs, liquidity, and risk, SLAS would lose mortgage servicing income.[6] In the long run they could at least partially offset the loss in income by reducing operating expenses. What seems fairly clear is the eventual near-complete usage of this limited authority by SLAS unless the home mortgage rate rises relative to the bond rate.[7]

The housing industry vehemently objected to this provision in the FIA because they feared it would result in massive short-run shifts into corporate bonds when bond yields rose. The past behavior of mutual savings banks gives credence to this fear. Mutual savings

---

[6] Insofar as the SLAS continued to originate the mortgages but then sold them to the FHLMC or FNMA, SLAS would retain the servicing income.

[7] If the financial reform legislation removes the present extraordinary provision for loan loss reserves currently granted thrifts, as the FIA of 1975 proposed to do, then a substantial shift (say 5 percent of total assets) of thrifts into tax-exempt securities could also be expected. Effective tax rates of thrifts are currently too low to make investment in tax-exempts profitable. On this topic, see Patric H. Hendershott, "An Analysis of the Expected Impact of the Financial Institutions Act of 1975," in Buckley, Tuccillo, and Villani, eds., *Capital Markets and the Housing Sector: Perspectives on Financial Reform* (Cambridge, Mass.: Ballinger Publishing Company, 1977), pp. 25–61.

banks shifted sharply away from home mortgages in the middle and late 1960s when bond yields rose relative to mortgage yields.

Given the strong opposition of the housing lobby to the diversification of SLAS into corporate debt, and the questionable value of the diversification to the viability of SLAS, this reform is unlikely to be contained in any successful financial reform legislation.

Variable-Rate Mortgages. Variable-rate mortgages (VRMS) have been proposed as a means of balancing the maturity of thrift portfolios without reducing the term to maturity of the mortgage instrument. They accomplish this objective by providing a long-term mortgage contract, amortized over as many as thirty years, with a provision for occasional rate adjustments. This provision is the fundamental difference between variable and fixed rate mortgages. The interest rate applicable to the loan balance of a VRM is tied to an index, typically an open-market rate such as that on Treasury bills or the thrift cost of funds. Allowable adjustments to the mortgage rate are usually limited in scope and frequency, typically to 25 basis points every six months and a maximum of 2½ percentage points over the life of the mortgage.

The primary objective of VRMS is to lessen the interest rate risk to thrift institution lenders of maturity intermediation without reducing thrift specialization in mortgages. Mortgage rates on existing VRMS would rise in concert with a general rise in interest rates such as occurred during the past decade. While the market value of VRMS would still decline if market rates rose more steeply than the VRM rate, the drop would be much less than that of fixed-rate mortgages. Thus, the widespread use of VRMS would reduce the periods of technical insolvency—when the market value of liabilities exceeds the market value of assets—such as that which threatened the viability of the entire industry in 1969 and made continued low deposit rate ceilings necessary. A related justification for the widespread use of VRMS is that they would improve thrift cash flow, increasing mortgage revenue when deposit rates are rising and decreasing it when deposit rates are falling.

There is, however, another side of the coin. The interest rate risk that thrifts would be avoiding with VRMS does not disappear; it is simply shifted to households. With fixed-rate mortgages, households are assured of nonrising monthly mortgage payments; with VRMS, the payments can rise. This is, of course, the reason for the dampers on the speed and total amount of the increase in the yields on VRMs.[8] The possible increase in monthly mortgage payments is illustrated in the following example. Assume that a household obtains a thirty-year, 10 percent down, $30,000 VRM at 5½ percent. Interest rates then rise rapidly so that five years later the household would be paying the maximum possible, 8 percent. The monthly payment of the household would, as a result, have risen from $170 to $217 or by 27 percent. If the rate had risen from 9 percent, the current level, to 11½ percent, then the monthly payment would have increased by almost 22 percent by the sixth year of the loan.

The Federal Home Loan Bank Board attempted to obtain congressional approval to authorize VRMs for federally chartered SLAs in the spring of 1975. Congress rebuffed this attempt, instead introducing legislation that would specifically forbid certain types of VRMs.[9] This extreme action reflected the concern that VRMs could shift an undue share of the interest rate risk to homeowners. Congressional opposition appears to be weakening as evidence is compiled from actual operating experience with VRMs. Currently, VRMs are authorized for state-chartered institutions in a limited number of states and are widespread in three—California, Hawaii, and Massachusetts. It should be noted, however, that there has been very little experience with actual increases in rates on existing VRMs. In California, where the bulk of the VRMs have been issued, the rate has been constant; in January 1977, the cost-of-funds index to which these VRMs are tied fell to an extent that almost required a downward adjustment in the rate on VRMs.

Historically, substantial semipermanent increases in interest rates that would have given rise to an increase in the yield on VRMs of over a percentage point have occurred only during periods of accelerating inflation when household nominal incomes were also accelerating. Consequently, *real* mortgage payments on VRMs will usually not rise anywhere near as much as nominal payments will when rates increase, and the rise will probably not be permanent. Consider the example provided earlier when the rate on VRMs rose from 5½ percent to 8 percent. This could have been the experience of a household unfortunate enough to take out a VRM in early 1965. As we noted, the

---

[8] In California, for example, the variable rate may not rise by more than ¼ percentage point during any semiannual period or 2½ percentage points during the life of the loan.

[9] This legislation was dropped when the FHLBB agreed not to issue the regulations permitting VRMs. A discussion of early congressional views on VRMs is contained in U.S. Congress, House of Representatives, Subcommittee on Financial Institutions, Supervision, Regulation, and Insurance of the Committee on Banking, Currency, and Housing, *Hearings on Variable Rate Mortgage Proposal and Regulation Q*, 94th Congress, 1st session, April 1975, pp. 1–4.

nominal payment would have been 27 percent higher in 1970. Given the nearly 25 percent increase in the consumer price index, the real monthly payment rose by only 2 percent. It is also instructive to trace that household's hypothetical experience through to the present. The substantial inflation between 1970 and 1976 would result in the real monthly mortgage payment being fully 35 percent below the original 1965 payment. Moreover, it is worth noting that the average cost of funds of savings and loans rose by less than a full percentage point between 1965 and 1970 and has risen by only about a percentage point since then. Thus, those with VRMs whose yield is tied to the cost of funds would probably have experienced a substantially slower rise in rate than that indicated in the example. (If thrifts had had substantial portions of their portfolios in VRMs, then the regulators of deposit rate ceilings would undoubtedly have raised the ceilings to enable the VRM-generated income of thrifts to be paid to depositors, resulting in a higher thrift cost of funds and thus a higher yield on existing VRMs. Thus, the full 2½ percentage point rise in the VRMs would likely have occurred by 1974, but at no time would the real monthly payment have exceeded that in 1965.)

The implication of these calculations—that VRMs are not as potentially harmful to households as some contend—is supported with data provided by S. R. Stansell and J. A. Millar on the variable-rate home mortgage program of the Federal Land Banks.[10] Between the middle of 1973 and the end of 1974, rates were raised in all states by between ¾ and 1¾ percentage points with the increase being 1½ percentage points in over half the states. Estimates of the ratio of the variable mortgage payment to personal income rose in only fourteen states and by more than ½ percentage point in only six. Between the end of 1972 and the end of 1974, an estimate of the ratio of the mortgage payment to per capita personal income increased in only four states and by more than ½ percentage point in only one.[11]

To summarize, households generally could have afforded the magnitude of increased monthly mortgage payments that would have occurred with VRMs during the 1965–1975 period. Households whose incomes rise with the inflation that accompanies rising interest rates are much better able to absorb interest rate risk than thrifts with imbalanced portfolios could in the absence of deposit rate ceilings.

---

[10] S. R. Stansell and J. A. Millar, "An Empirical Study of Mortgage Payments to Income Ratios in a Variable Rate Mortgage Program," *Journal of Finance*, May 1976, pp. 415–25.

[11] The one large increase, Tennessee, appears to be due to an error in the datum for the end of 1972. Similarly, the largest increase in the earlier estimates seems to be due to an error in the mid-1973 datum for Minnesota.

Extended Liability Authorities

The strictures on liability authorities of thrifts are far less severe than those on asset powers. The major limitation has been a ban on thrift checking accounts. Nonetheless, a detailed analysis of why thrifts have not increased the maturity of their liabilities more than they have is of interest because thrifts could reduce or eliminate their asset-liability maturity imbalance by either lengthening their liabilities or shortening their assets. Checking accounts, long-term deposits, and other long-term liabilities are considered in turn. The primary emphasis will be on the ability of these powers to balance the maturity of thrift asset and liability portfolios and to increase mortgage lending.

Checking Accounts. All recent reform packages have contained provisions for thrifts to receive authority to issue demand and/or negotiated order of withdrawal (NOW) accounts. NOWs, while paying interest and officially classified as savings accounts, also serve as checking accounts and thus are ideal from the consumer's viewpoint. The motivations underlying the granting of NOW authority to commercial banks and thrifts seem to be three. First, both the payment of interest and the increased competition between commercial banks and thrifts are likely to provide substantial benefits to households. Second, this authority puts thrifts on a more equal basis with commercial banks who previously had a monopoly on checking accounts. Third, insofar as thrifts obtain more funds and continue to invest a larger share of them in residential mortgages than do commercial banks, NOWs will increase the supply of funds for housing. The first of these points is obvious and thus will not be discussed further. The impact of NOWs on thrifts and housing is of greater interest.

Thrifts appear to view NOWs much as they do consumer credit: as a means to become "family financial centers." We see them in a similar light. If thrifts are to be able to compete on an equal basis with commercial banks for household savings, then they must be able to provide the same set of services to households that commercial banks do. Possibly the most important of these is checking accounts.

The present general lack of enthusiasm of thrifts for this authority is probably an accurate gauge of the profitability of NOWs.[12]

---

[12] See, for example, the testimony of Lloyd S. Bowles and Norman Strunk on behalf of the U.S. League before the U.S. Congress, Senate, Subcommittee on Financial Institutions of the Committee on Banking, Housing, and Urban Affairs, *Hearings on NOW Accounts, Federal Reserve Membership, and Related Issues*, 95th Congress, 1st session, June 1977, pp. 177–223. Another reason for the unenthusiasm of thrifts is a fear that reception of NOW authority would be accompanied by removal of the extra ¼ percentage point thrifts can offer depositors relative to what commercial banks can offer.

NOWS are not inexpensive funds like noninterest-bearing demand deposits of commercial banks. Moreover, thrift costs of handling these accounts could well be higher than those of commercial banks because of the generally smaller scale of thrift operations and less direct access to the check-processing facilities of the Federal Reserve system and private firms. Thus, we should not expect this authority to increase the profitability of thrifts (and it obviously worsens the maturity imbalance of thrift portfolios). Nonetheless, we would anticipate substantial interest of thrifts in NOWS if deposit rate ceilings were raised and thrifts were attempting to retain their share of the savings-account market.

We now turn to the likely magnitude of the growth in NOW accounts and demand deposits at thrifts and the expected impact on mortgage funds. In August 1973 Congress passed a law authorizing depository institutions other than credit unions in Massachusetts and New Hampshire to issue NOW accounts. (MSBS began offering these accounts in 1972, but the legality of this action was not clearly demonstrated until the federal legislation.) This authorization was extended to all of New England in March 1976 and to New York (noninterest-paying NOWS) in March 1977. (New Jersey and Pennsylvania were included in a preliminary version of the bill.)

The experiment in Massachusetts and New Hampshire has been in operation long enough to make some tentative estimates regarding the share of the checking-account market that would be captured by thrifts.[13] John D. Paulus has estimated that most of the growth in NOWS (80 percent) has been at the expense of commercial bank demand deposits rather than of savings accounts at either commercial banks or thrifts and that the growth in NOWS at commercial banks and at thrifts have not differed significantly in this regard.[14] Thus, simple comparison of the division of NOWS between commercial banks and thrifts would be a useful starting point.

The proportion of NOWS at thrifts in Massachusetts and New Hampshire are given in Table 11 for the end of 1975, mid-1976, and the end of 1976. As can be seen, the proportion is dropping in both states, but at a much slower rate in New Hampshire. It would

---

[13] For an excellent discussion of the competition for NOWS in Massachusetts and New Hampshire (and in the rest of New England in the very early months), see Ralph C. Kimball, "Recent Developments in the NOW Account Experiment in New England," *New England Economic Review*, November/December 1976, pp. 3-19.

[14] John D. Paulus, "Effects of 'NOW' Accounts on Costs and Earnings of Commercial Banks in 1974-75," *Staff Economic Study*, Federal Reserve Board, Summer 1976, pp. 9-11.

TABLE 11

PROPORTION OF NOWS AT THRIFTS
(in percentage points)

Date	Massachusetts	New Hampshire
end 1975	60	41
mid-1976	49	38
end 1976	44	36

SOURCE: Federal Reserve Bank of Boston.

appear likely that the thrift share of the NOW market, and eventually of the total checking-account market, will level out at about 35 percent. But, owing to their relatively large number of branches, thrifts in Massachusetts and New Hampshire are significantly more successful in attracting savings accounts than thrifts in the rest of the United States. In 1975, thrifts in these two states had 83 percent of time and savings accounts other than large certificates of deposits of individuals, proprietorships, and corporations (IPCs); in the rest of the United States, thrifts had only 55 percent. Thus, the 35 percent figure may be too high for the entire nation. If the ratio of the thrift share of NOW accounts to the thrift share of time and savings accounts is the same nationwide as it is in Massachusetts and New Hampshire, then thrifts will attract only 25 percent of the NOW market nationwide. This is slightly less than half of the 60 percent of the household savings-account market that they now have.

Even a 25 percent share of the checking-account market at the end of 1976 would result in $20 billion in new deposits for thrifts. If these funds are invested as savings accounts are, then 60 percent or $12 billion would flow into home mortgages.

Long-Term Deposits. Thrift maturity imbalance originated as a by-product of liquidity intermediation. Mortgage borrowers preferred long-term mortgages, but small savers preferred a safe, liquid asset for their incremental savings. Thrifts facilitated the savings-investment process by accepting low-denomination deposits and providing virtually complete liquidity to savers while simultaneously making long-term mortgage loans. There was no consideration of the interest rate risk involved when this process originated because interest rates were relatively stable and the dearth of available open-market investments gave stability to deposit flows. The sharp rise and increased volatility in interest rates and the growth in open-market investments during the past decade have reduced the ability of thrifts to accept the interest rate risk of maturity intermediation.

As noted in chapter 4, thrifts have responded with substantial issues of four- and six-year deposits. Thrifts have been limited in issuing longer-term deposits by a combination of regulations and events. Deposit rate ceilings apply to accounts under $100,000. The maximum rate allowable is 7.75 percent, and this rate applies to all accounts with maturities of six years or more (in the middle of 1978 an 8 percent ceiling was introduced on accounts with maturity of eight or more years). Whenever the ceiling is binding on six-year certificates and the term structure of interest rates is upward sloping beyond six years, thrifts are effectively precluded from issuing deposits with maturities greater than six years.[15] The lifting of deposit rate ceilings on longer-term certificates would lead to greater issues of them.

Donald P. Tucker proposes further that the current $1,000 minimum balance requirement and the stiff penalties for premature withdrawal be modified.[16] The minimum deposit requirement discourages incremental additions to existing accounts and makes it particularly difficult for the small saver who has not yet accumulated the necessary $1,000 minimum to take advantage of the higher yield. Premature withdrawals, even if they occur shortly before the account matures, impose substantial penalties on the saver.[17] While setting minimum requirements obviously reduces costs of servicing the accounts and thus allows thrifts to pay higher deposit rates, lower balance accounts could be offered profitably at lower interest rates.

The expansion of long-term deposits at thrifts depends on household demand for long-term higher yielding securities and the supply of comparable securities offered by commercial banks and others. Many households have accumulated substantial wealth in savings accounts and require liquidity only for a small portion of this savings. This is one reason why deposits with maturities of four or more years

---

[15] Salomon Brothers data on yields on agency securities suggest that the yield curve was downward sloping in the five-to-ten year range from June 1969 to February 1970 and again from July to September in 1974. During these periods it should have been easier for thrifts to market ten-year accounts than either four- or six-year accounts.

[16] Donald P. Tucker, "Financial Innovation and the Mortgage Market: The Possibilities for Liability Management by Thrifts," *Journal of Finance*, May 1976, pp. 427–37 (and "Discussion," pp. 441–43).

[17] This loss can be sharply reduced by borrowing short term at a slightly higher rate until the deposit certificate matures.

currently account for about 35 percent of thrift deposits. Another reason is the extension of the tax advantages of retirement savings to millions of households not previously covered. Currently, an individual can deposit up to $1,500 in an individual retirement account (IRA) or $7,500 in a Keough retirement account per year. The tax laws impose substantial penalties for premature withdrawals from such accounts, so liquidity is not an important feature to these investors.

The second issue is the extent to which other borrowers will compete for these funds. There is currently a dearth of small or medium denominations in intermediate and long-term securities with federal guarantees. Congress has imposed a ceiling rate on Treasury bonds, effectively precluding the Treasury from issuing them (occasional minor exceptions have been made). GNMA pass-through securities have grown rapidly, but are sold only in minimum denominations of $25,000. Similarly, the FHLBB and FNMA have been issuing securities in the intermediate and longer maturity range, but in minimum denominations of $10,000.

Commercial banks are the largest potential competitor for long-term deposits. Thrifts currently have a greater share of long-term certificates than passbook deposits, but it is not clear whether this is due to supply or demand factors. But if commercial banks continue to invest primarily in short-term bank loans and thrifts in longer-term mortgages, then banks will compete more vigorously for the shorter-term deposits and thrifts for the longer-term deposits as both attempt to reduce interest rate risk.

The final issue is the extent to which the removal of rate ceilings and reduction in minimum deposit requirements and in penalties for premature withdrawal would allow thrifts to lengthen the maturity of their deposits. If favorable assumptions are made regarding household demand and bank competition, a conceivable outcome is an equal distribution of accounts between, for example, maturities of zero, two, four, six, eight, and ten years. This would result in an average maturity of *new* accounts of about five years. The average maturity of outstanding debt would be only half that, or two and a half years. Given an average effective maturity of new home mortgage loans of ten years and an average maturity of a portfolio of loans of about five, it is clear that long-term deposits cannot singlehandedly balance the thrift portfolio and eliminate interest rate risk. Rather, they represent one path available to the industry to reduce this risk exposure.

Other Long-Term Liabilities. Several recent financial innovations, specifically the authority for thrifts to issue mortgage-backed bonds

(MBBS) and long-term subordinated debt (LTSD), allow for lengthening of the liability structure of SLAS. The issuance of LTSD has been authorized since early 1973; authorization for MBBS came in the spring of 1975. The LTSD authority allows thrifts to issue debt in the marketplace as nonfinancial corporations and commercial banks presently do.

In addition to lengthening the maturity of the thrift portfolio, LTSD offers several advantages over other forms of debt. LTSD is actually counted as equity capital by many financial analysts because of its distant maturity and subordination. Thus, it may improve the flexibility and profitability of thrift operations for several reasons. First, federal tax law favors the issue of LTSD over equity (interest payments are deductible, but dividend payments are not). Second, current FSLIC requirements of minimum additions to reserves impinge on the ability of thrifts to pursue an investment strategy that sacrifices current earnings for even greater future earnings. Volatile earnings were seen to be an unavoidable consequence of maturity intermediation in chapter 2. This volatility follows from cyclical short-term interest costs and stable long-term mortgage revenues. Thus, when short-term rates are high, current earnings may be insufficient to meet FSLIC requirements for net additions to reserves. The ability to meet these requirements through LTSD issues could improve the long-term profitability of the industry by facilitating maturity intermediation.

The issue of LTSD has been limited by several factors. First, it is a risky investment. For institutions with mutual charters, the claims of LTSD holders are subordinated to the claims of all others. LTSD thus contains all of the downside risk of equity investment in a highly leveraged firm, with no additional reward for successful performance. Second, most thrift institutions are small and unknown in the capital markets. Thus, their borrowing rate will include a relatively large risk premium.

Although the authority to issue mortgage-backed bonds is a more recent development, MBBS have received more widespread attention and support than LTSD, as evidenced by the numerous articles on this subject in the FHLBB *Journal*.[18] The only substantial difference between these instruments is the risk to the investor. By definition, subordinated debentures are an unsecured instrument and, thus, investors in such debentures would stand behind holders of MBBS in the event of failure by an SLA. Because the proceeds from the liquidation of assets are independent of whether they were financed with

---

[18] In 1975 alone, there were six articles dealing with mortgage-backed bonds.

LTSD or MBBS, it is clear that some of the risk of MBBS is being transferred. The FSLIC, which insures virtually 100 percent of deposits, ultimately bears this risk. The transfer of risk to the FSLIC occurs because the value of mortgages pledged as collateral against MBBS has exceeded the value of the MBBS by 50 to 110 percent in order to receive the favorable Aaa securities rating.[19] Moreover, the least risky (FHA/VA-insured) mortgages of the thrifts are often pledged. Conceptually, should an SLA issue several overcollateralized MBBS, the par value of its uncollateralized mortgage holdings could fall below the par value of insured deposits. If the SLA then failed, because of a sharp upward movement in interest rates or whatever, the FSLIC would have to make up the difference. It would thus be appropriate for the FSLIC to issue regulations prohibiting the overcollateralization of MBBS. Instead, FSLIC should insure the MBBS directly and charge a premium for the insurance.

The primary factor limiting MBB issues is the yield differential between bonds and mortgages. SLAS find it difficult to originate a mortgage pool at rates that are held down by the activities of the credit agencies, cover their origination and servicing expenses, and have enough remaining revenue to pay the going bond rate. The rise in mortgage rates relative to bond rates in 1977 allowed the profitable issuance of MBBS.

Interest Rate Risk Insurance

Current financial market regulation and intervention influence both the costs and the revenues of thrift institutions. It follows that changes in market regulation and/or intervention would have an impact on the pattern and level of thrift industry profitability. We have thus far considered reforms and market intervention that impact on thrift revenues (liberalized asset powers and agency activities) and costs (liberalized liability powers and increases in deposit rate ceilings). There is another alternative, the direct stabilization of thrift revenues and net worth. The principal proposal with this intent is interest rate risk insurance.

SLAS provide a form of interest rate risk insurance to households by making fixed-rate mortgage funds available. Homeowners are insured against increases in mortgage borrowing costs and monthly payments that result from increases in interest rates generally and in

---

[19] This information and the manner in which MBBS are rated is provided in "Fixed Income Investor," Standard & Poor's Corp., vol. 5, no. 50, section 2 (1977), pp. 1–15.

the cost of funds financing their loans specifically. Given the relatively short-term liability structure of SLAS, they can ill afford to provide this insurance. The risk to SLAS has, of course, been sharply reduced in the current financial structure by ceilings on deposit rates.

Numerous proposals have been advanced for the establishment of an insurance corporation to insure this risk. All proposals for interest rate risk insurance (IRRI) share one common feature; the insurer makes payments to the lender in response to a rise in an index tied to market interest rates, and lenders pay the insurer when the index falls. The IRRI concept is appealing because it addresses the fundamental risk problem of maturity imbalance at thrifts without requiring households to absorb this risk by giving up fixed-payment mortgages.

Profitable intermediation of any kind consists of lending at rates sufficiently above borrowing costs to cover the costs of intermediation. Opportunities for this exist because of differences in the types of securities economic units wish to purchase and issue. Assume that (1) the current lending rate for fixed-payment mortgages is rl, (2) the thrift calculates it must net x percent on its portfolio to cover operating expenses and earn a normal rate of return (for stock companies), and (3) the average effective deposit rate the thrift expects to pay over the effective life of the mortgage is rd^e. If the life of the mortgage and future deposit rates were known with certainty, then an SLA should make the mortgage loan whenever $rl \geq rd^e + x$. Under these circumstances the SLA still could experience the cash flow difficulties described in chapter 2 (the deposit rate might be relatively high early in the life of the mortgage investment), but long-run losses from unexpected interest rate shifts would not occur.

Realistically, there is substantial uncertainty regarding both the life of the individual mortgage and future deposit rates (in a world without rate ceilings). Risk-averse discretionary investors will require compensation, known as the liquidity premium in the literature on the term structure of interest rates, for assuming this risk. The new decision rule is, if $rl \geq rd^e + x + l$, where l is the liquidity premium, then the loan should be made. If competitive markets exist, then mortgage and deposit rates will adjust until $rl = rd^e + x + l$. Thrifts lose money on mortgages for which the actual effective deposit cost over the life of the mortgage exceeds the expected cost plus the liquidity premium ($rd^e + l$). When the actual cost falls below the expected cost, thrifts will earn higher profits than expected.

Thrifts diversify away much of their default risk by purchasing a large number of mortgages issued by different households. Unfortunately, interest rate risk cannot be similarly reduced through diversification because all similar maturity loans made at the same time carry the same lending rate based on the same expected deposit rates. In plain English, if the thrift loses money on just one mortgage because of deposit rates rising unexpectedly, then it loses money on all mortgages that were made at the same time.

The thrift is in a somewhat better position to diversify risk over time. If forecasts are correct on average but wrong in individual years, excess profits in some years will offset losses in other years. However, if the lending rate remains below the actual effective deposit rate plus the markup to cover operating expenses for several consecutive years, then the viability of the institution will be threatened. The ability to avoid bankruptcy during the bad years depends on the accumulation of reserves in profitable years and the availability of advances.

A pure IRRI scheme would have the insurer making payments to SLAS when actual effective deposit rates rose above rates expected at the time a mortgage was made and SLAS making payments to the insurer when the reverse was true (a precise scheme is described in the Appendix). While SLAS are no longer subject to interest rate risk, the insurer bears the same risk SLAS previously bore and can no more diversify interest rate risk than SLAS could. Net benefit/premium payments would rise and fall with interest rates simultaneously for all insured SLAS. Because private insurers could not provide the requisite cash outflow if the general level of interest rates increased, federal sponsorship of IRRI is necessary.

There are a number of reasons why federal IRRI is likely to lead to substantial net federal outlays over time. First, post-World War II experience is one of almost continual underforecasting of future interest rates. If this pattern continues, mortgage rates will not cover the costs of intermediation and of deposit funds over the life of the mortgage. Second, even if future deposit costs were forecast accurately, SLA portfolio restrictions, combined with the activities of the federally sponsored credit agencies, act to hold mortgage rates down relative to other long-term rates, and thus mortgage rates will not fully reflect future expected deposit rates. The expectations theory of the term structure depends on the ability of investors to switch between short and long securities until long yields are consistent with expected future short-term yields. Such substitution is not possible for most mortgage lenders. Moreover, when interest rates decline, mortgages that were issued at earlier higher rates are likely to be paid off and refinanced, causing a shortfall in mortgage interest income.

A third reason is more subtle. If complete interest rate risk insurance were provided, thrifts, especially mutually chartered institutions, would have an incentive to offer low mortgage rates and high deposit rates. This would entail a subsidy to both borrowers and depositors. While this problem could be addressed by requiring thrifts to coinsure interest rate risk (see the Appendix for an illustration), such a plan would increase the administrative costs of IRRI.

Before concluding, it is useful to note an earlier alternative proposal for handling the cash flow and risk problems of thrifts, in the absence of deposit rate ceilings. When current profits are insufficient both to meet requirements of the Federal Savings and Loan Insurance Corporation (FSLIC) for additions to reserves and to finance a "market rate of interest" on deposits,[20] George G. Kaufman suggested that the FHLB system make sufficient advances available for these purposes.[21] This would be a subtle alteration of the existing advances mechanism. FHLB advances are currently used extensively to provide liquidity to the industry, as indicated by the countercyclical pattern of the outstanding stock of advances described earlier. Other evidence indicates that, except perhaps in capital-short western states, advances have not, at least until very recently, been used to finance a permanent expansion of mortgage lending. The fundamental change implied by the Kaufman proposal is in the origin and purpose of the demand for liquidity. Deposit rate ceilings currently give rise to a countercyclical demand to offset slowdowns in deposit growth, whereas removal of the ceilings would generate the same pattern of demand to pay higher dividends on savings shares. In the latter case, costs go up so reserves decline.

A comparison of IRRI with the Kaufman advances proposal is interesting. In terms of the thrifts, potential cash outlays when interest rates rise are met by insurance benefits (an asset), rather than advances (a liability). In this way, SLA net worth is stabilized (the insolvency and cash flow problems are solved simultaneously). From the perspective of the capital markets, under IRRI Treasury securities substitute for FHLB securities.

[20] FSLIC currently requires that SLAS make annual net additions to reserves. To improve SLA operating flexibility, the FSLIC could grant explicit recognition to the natural volatility of thrift earnings and gear its reserves policy accordingly. Total requirements for net additions to reserves could be set for longer time horizons, for example five years, or possibly even over the interest-rate cycle itself. Wide—but not unlimited—latitude could be allowed within this time horizon for intermediate reserve goals.

[21] George G. Kaufman, "A Proposal for Eliminating Interest-Rate Ceilings on Thrift Institutions, A Comment," *Journal of Money, Credit, and Banking,* August 1972, pp. 735–43.

Summary

The necessity of regulating the deposit market by preventing rate competition stems from the competitive advantages (consumer credit and demand deposit authorities) enjoyed by commercial banks and the asset/liability imbalance of thrifts. If thrifts are to be viable when deposit rate ceilings are raised, then the advantages of banks must be eliminated and restrictions prohibiting thrift portfolio balance must be removed.

Competitive parity with banks requires that thrifts be able to offer the same financial services to households. Currently, commercial banks enjoy two legislated advantages, checking accounts and consumer loans. Consumers highly value the convenience offered by "one stop banking," so this distinction between banks and thrifts must be removed. Although the provision of these services is not likely to generate large profits, especially at smaller thrifts, both are necessary for thrifts to become "family financial centers."

The current inability of thrifts to pay competitive short-term deposit rates during periods of relatively high interest rates stems from thrift specialization in long-term fixed-rate mortgages. Proposals to overcome this problem by allowing thrifts to leave the mortgage market (for example, the authority to invest in corporate debt) come under heavy criticism from housing proponents. Moreover, the maturity imbalance problem is tied to the fixed-rate mortgage instrument, not mortgage investment generally. Variable-rate mortgages address the specific problem by shortening the effective term of the contract with respect to the interest rate. VRMs, in combination with longer-term deposits, could balance thrift portfolios sufficiently to support competition with commercial banks without requiring a diversion of funds from the mortgage market. Another method of balancing thrift portfolios would be substantial issues of bonds to be used to finance mortgage purchases. The reduction in the mortgage rate relative to the bond rate engineered by the federal agencies has rendered such actions unprofitable except when extraordinary mortgage issues relative to bond issues offset the impact of the agencies.

One problem with VRMs is that they transfer interest rate risk to mortgage borrowers. VRM opponents argue that households are less able to bear this risk than thrifts. In fact, the reverse seems to be true. Because significant increases in interest rates are almost certain to be accompanied by rising inflation rates, household nominal incomes tend to increase when monthly payments on variable-rate mortgages are rising. Thus real monthly payments are unlikely to increase significantly except for quite brief intervals. Moreover, as long as both fixed- and variable-rate options are available in the marketplace, those borrowers with better income prospects during inflationary periods will be more likely to issue a VRM.

Because the controversy over this risk transfer has in the past given rise to congressional opposition to VRMs, we considered interest rate risk insurance (IRRI) as an alternative to portfolio balance. Such insurance requires federal sponsorship because it could necessitate long-term negative cash flows. IRRI could protect thrift viability as well as (or perhaps, better than) VRMs over the rate cycle. But this approach represents a less desirable alternative because it will almost certainly result in federal subsidies. Thrifts will have an incentive to offer low rates to mortgagees and high rates to depositors; that is, to manage portfolios so as to maximize benefits and minimize premiums. The safeguards against these practices increase the complexity of the insurance approach and make it more difficult to administer. IRRI should be considered only if the maturity balance approach is politically unacceptable.

8

Ensuring the Long-Run Viability of Primary Investors in Home Mortgages

One of the important responses to the 1965–1970 rise in interest rates was the expansion of the role of the federally sponsored agencies in the home mortgage market. The intention was to protect housing from bearing a disproportionately large share of the burden of inflation and rising interest rates. As was emphasized in chapter 3, the response was effective in mitigating the rise in the home mortgage rate. The reduction in yields on home mortgages relative to those on other open-market securities is the second greatest obstacle to financial reform (the greatest being the required maturity imbalance of thrift portfolios). If thrifts are more heavily invested in low-yielding home mortgages than commercial banks are, then thrifts will not be able to offer as high deposit rates as commercial banks can. Even if the maturity imbalance problem is successfully handled, thrifts will still be at a long-run competitive disadvantage. Similarly, if some banks (small?) are more heavily invested in home mortgages than are others (large?), then the former will be at a disadvantage relative to the latter.

The simplest solution to the problem of below-market home mortgage rates is to place a cap on the direct and indirect mortgage holdings of the federal government and its sponsored credit agencies and let the mortgage rate seek its free-market level. In addition to putting thrifts on a competitive basis with commercial banks, the resultant rise in home mortgage rates would lead to a more efficient allocation of resources. Keeping the home mortgage rate a half percentage point below the free-market rate biases the capital stock of the economy in favor of housing and away from other forms of investment. And this bias is in addition to that induced by the failure to tax the return on equity invested in one's home.

If politicians are reluctant to allow the cost of mortgage credit to rise, then three alternative means are available to prevent depositors from bearing the burden of low mortgage rates and to enable thrifts to compete successfully over the long-run with commercial banks for deposits. A credit allocation scheme could be employed whereby commercial banks are required to invest as heavily as thrifts in home mortgages; thrifts could be permitted to shift out of mortgages and into the higher-yielding other assets; and thrifts could be given a subsidy sufficient to raise the effective yield on home mortgages to a level equivalent to that on other assets.

Credit Allocation Schemes

The government could require thrifts (and create credit agencies with a sufficient profit incentive) to purchase enough mortgages to drive the home mortgage rate down by the desired amount. The level of required purchases must be close to that of all new issues of home mortgages, because the lower home mortgage rate would cause institutions not required to hold mortgages to fail to replace their holdings when they mature. If thrift mortgage investment does not absorb the former market share of discretionary lenders, then the home mortgage rate would rise to its initial level.

This system should be familiar because a close facsimile presently exists. Thrifts are effectively required to purchase large quantities of home mortgages through the restrictions placed on their investments in other securities (corporate debt and consumer credit), federally sponsored credit agencies have accumulated large mortgage portfolios, and discretionary investors, particularly life insurance companies and pension funds, have been liquidating their holdings. The problem here is that requiring thrifts to invest in a low-yielding asset limits the amount that they can pay their depositors and thus the extent to which they can compete for deposits with commercial banks. These are precisely the features of the financial system that reform is supposed to alter.

Alternatively, commercial banks or pension funds could be required to buy mortgages. The House Committee on Banking, Finance, and Urban Affairs has considered allocation requirements for commercial banks, and the National Association of Home Builders (NAHB) annually proposes legislation requiring pension fund participation in the residential mortgage market.[1] But here, too, bank depositors will receive lower income, or participants in pension funds

---

[1] See, for example, the statement of the NAHB Board of Directors, "Housing— A Common Sense Program," May 23, 1976, which took the position that pension

will receive reduced benefits. To illustrate the latter, if the return on the investment portfolio of a pension fund were permanently reduced by 1 percentage point, a forty-year-old would suffer a one-fifth decline in the benefits he can expect to receive after his retirement at age sixty-five and a twenty-year-old would suffer over a 30 percent decline.[2]

A broad credit allocation scheme would have the advantage over the present system of spreading the costs of the lower home mortgage rates across holders of the liabilities of many institutions, rather than just those holding thrift accounts; however, it would also have numerous disadvantages. First, there would be a strong incentive for borrowers to issue residential mortgages to finance investments other than residential construction. The proportion of residential construction financed (the loan-to-value ratio) would rise, and some very unusual investments would be classified as residential property or would be combined with it so that they, too, could be used to meet the required investment standard. The net result would be a larger dollar cost of lower mortgage rates (the same reduction in the rate multiplied by a larger stock of mortgages) to be spread among holders of liabilities at financial institutions. Second, there are the costs of administration of an allocation program. These include the costs of the institutions in complying with the regulations and of the regulatory agencies in monitoring both the institutions, to ensure compliance, and the issuers of mortgages, to limit issues for nonhousing purposes. Third, there are the inefficiencies (or costs) introduced by requiring institutions that had not previously invested in mortgages to do so. Such institutions do not have the expertise needed to invest efficiently in these markets. All of the above costs would be borne by either the holders of the liabilities of the financial institutions or the taxpayers. On balance, alternative allocation schemes do not appear to be any more promising than the present one.

Federalization of the Home Mortgage Market

An alternative to the present system of holding down home mortgage rates is complete federalization of the home mortgage market. As noted in chapter 3, federal direct and indirect mortgage purchases for the most part simply replaced (or drove out) purchases by discre-

---

funds be required to invest a portion of assets in residential mortgages in order for them to retain their income tax exemption privileges. This has been a part of the NAHB legislative platform for years.

[2] Irwin Tepper and A.R.P. Affleck, "Pension Plan Liabilities and Corporate Financial Strategies," *Journal of Finance*, December 1974, pp. 1549–64.

tionary investors. Removal of restrictions on SLA portfolios would allow SLAs to become discretionary investors and avoid the cost of low home mortgage rates. Federalization of the mortgage market could be accomplished by replacing thrifts in the mortgage market with expanded agency activity, including mortgage pools, or direct Treasury investment sufficient to drive mortgage rates down to the desired level.

Although legislation for complete federalization of the mortgage market has never been openly proposed in Congress, it has been attempted indirectly through the continued expansion of the role of the agencies. Senator William Proxmire (D–Wis.), chairman of the Senate Committee on Banking, Housing, and Urban Affairs, stated that there was no time during the past decade when it has been appropriate for FNMA to sell mortgages.[3] Similar sentiments exist in the House, as evidenced by the House version of financial reform sponsored by Representative Fernand St Germain (D–R.I.) that called, indirectly, for a vast expansion of FHLB direct lending to finance thrift mortgage lending at below market rates.[4]

Because the Treasury can borrow more cheaply in the capital markets than can private investors, proponents of federalization argue that it is relatively costless. It is true that the Treasury will not bear any direct cost insofar as its borrowing rate does not exceed the subsidized mortgage rate, but this is because the direct cost of the below-market mortgage rate is passed on to others, as will be shown. Moreover, to the extent that the Treasury borrowing rate rises, costs will be incurred in the form of higher interest payments on the existing outstanding Treasury debt.

Calculation of the costs to the Treasury requires the general specification of the relationship between yields in unregulated financial markets. If interest income from home mortgages and from Treasury securities are taxed equally, the home mortgage rate (Rmor) would exceed the yield on a Treasury security (Rus) by, all on an annual percentage basis, the marginal cost of servicing mortgages (s), the expected cost of delinquencies and foreclosures (f), a risk premium (r), a liquidity premium (l), and a marketability premium (m). Thus

---

[3] U.S. Congress, Senate, Committee on Banking, Housing, and Urban Affairs, *Secondary Market Operations of the Federal National Mortgage Association and the Federal Home Loan Mortgage Corporation*, 94th Congress, pp. 186–89.
[4] U.S. Congress, House of Representatives, Subcommittee on Financial Institutions Supervision, Regulation, and Insurance, Committee on Banking, Currency, and Housing, *The Financial Reform Act of 1976*, 94th Congress, 2nd session, March 1976.

$$Rmor = Rus + s + f + r + l + m. \tag{1}$$

The premiums reflect the costs of inducing investors to hold mortgages with uncertain delinquency and foreclosure rates, with a long term to maturity, and with a thin secondary market. The conclusion that federalization of the home mortgage market (the issuance of securities and purchase of the mortgage stock) is costless to the government rests on the premise that the government may earn the risk, liquidity, and marketability premiums and pass them along to households with no increase in the Treasury borrowing rate. Note that the government does not gain anything on the servicing and foreclosure components, s and f. While the government's mortgage interest income reflects them, the government as holder of the mortgages must also pay for the servicing and accept the occasional delays in and absence of mortgage payments.

The risk, liquidity, and marketability premiums reflect market prices to induce lenders to accept debt instruments that are risky, illiquid, and less than perfectly marketable. Because these premiums decline in response to the increased supply of Treasury securities, the spread between the mortgage and Treasury rates falls. To see this, it is useful to examine the underpinnings of these premiums and the process by which federalization eliminates them.

The ex post return on the average mortgage portfolio is uncertain because actual default and foreclosure losses are unknown. The distribution of these losses may be deduced from past experience. The expected loss is represented by f, the mean or average value of the distribution of default and foreclosure costs. If the average mortgage investor is averse to the risk that his default experience will exceed f, then he will demand a positive risk premium (r) to compensate for this risk.[5] (A risk taker, in contrast, would accept a negative premium for the riskier security in the pursuit of below-average default and foreclosure losses.)

Investors with varying degrees of risk aversion participate in the financial markets. The market determined value of r is the premium just sufficient to attract the marginal risk-averse investor from the riskless to the risky market. As federalization proceeds, however, the Treasury replaces risky mortgage securities with riskless federal securities in the portfolios of increasingly less risk-averse investors

---

[5] The ex post return on a mortgage portfolio is also uncertain owing to the possibility that the mortgage could be called by the issuer (repaid early) in response to a decline in interest rates and the repaid funds would have to be reinvested at a lower yield. The risk premium will also reflect this risk, but we shall ignore this complication.

(those with increasingly lower r's). In the limit, the marginal liquidator of mortgages will probably attach no special value to the riskless characteristic of Treasury securities; r will be zero.

Treasury securities are more marketable than mortgages. Thus investors needing the ability to sell a security on short notice tend to invest in Treasury securities rather than mortgages.[6] The value mortgage investors attach to marketability varies widely. Many past and present participants in the mortgage market attach little value. To illustrate, life insurance companies replaced marketable FHA/VA mortgages largely with nonmarketable directly placed corporate bonds and multifamily and commercial mortgages. Moreover, when the need arises for a mortgage investor to sell, the secondary market facilities of the FNMA and FHLMC and the direct placement services of the AMINET computer system can be employed. Nonetheless, the current marketability premium determined by marginal mortgage-market investors is significant. As federalization of the mortgage market proceeds, the Treasury replaces less marketable mortgages with marketable Treasury securities in the portfolios of investors with less and less need for marketability (with lower m's). Again in the limit the marginal investor will probably attach no special value to the highly marketable characteristic of Treasury securities; m will be zero.

The distribution of securities among various maturities and the liquidity premium reflect the behavior of both borrowers and lenders. Borrowers prefer to issue securities with a maturity close to the life of the asset they are financing; a bond or mortgage for a structure and an intermediate term loan for producers' and consumers' durables. Borrowing either shorter or longer term than the life of the asset might result in borrowing costs that differ from those expected when the investment was made. Borrowing shorter term is particularly undesirable because it creates the possibility of having to refinance at an inopportune moment. Households save and lend for a variety of purposes over a variety of time horizons. They like to hold very short-term assets for basic liquidity needs, intermediate assets when accumulating a downpayment on a house or tuition for future college years, and long-term assets for a distant retirement.[7] Because financial investors prefer, on the average, to hold shorter-term financial

---

[6] The popularity of GNMA mortgage pools is evidence of the desirability of marketability and dislike of risk on the part of both traditional and nontraditional mortgage investors.

[7] This assumes the absence of substantial uncertainty regarding future inflation. If investors view accelerating inflation as a significant possibility, then they will tend to invest shorter term to reduce the uncertainty regarding real rates of return. This would raise the liquidity premium.

TABLE 12

ACTUAL AND HYPOTHETICAL YIELDS ON LONG-TERM DEBT
(in percentage points)

	Actual	Hypothetical	
		Free Market	Federalization
Home mortgages (less service fees)	8.75	9.25	8.60
Corporate (Aa) bonds	8.50	8.25	8.60
Treasury bonds	8.00	7.65	8.35

claims than borrowers wish to issue, long-term borrowers have to pay a liquidity premium to induce investors to buy their issues, although empirical evidence suggests that only the very shortest-term (less than three-month) borrowers avoid paying a significant premium.[8]

If the Treasury replaces mortgages with debt of comparable maturity, then it will not earn the liquidity premium. Alternatively, short-term financing of the necessary magnitude will erode the liquidity premium as these securities are substituted for long-term securities in portfolios of investors with shorter holding periods. To issue more and more short-term securities will eventually require the Treasury to pay a premium to induce investors with longer-term holding periods to accept short-term government securities, that is, the liquidity premium would become negative. This result can be avoided only by issuing a wide variety of debt instruments with maturities that match the holding periods of all investors in the marketplace. In this case the liquidity premium disappears as federalization of the mortgage market proceeds.

Some actual and hypothetical interest rates that might exist under alternative scenarios are presented in Table 12. The first column contains a close approximation to late 1977 interest rates on long-term debt claims. The home mortgage and corporate bond (Aa rated)

---

[8] Assuming that all future expected short-term rates equal the current one, it has been estimated that the three-month rate would exceed the one-day rate by 34 basis points, that the one-year rate would exceed the three-month rate by 9 basis points, but that all maturities one year and longer would have equal yields (J. H. McCulloch, "An Estimate of the Liquidity Premium," *Journal of Political Economy*, February 1975, pp. 112–13). If the liquidity premium were taken to be the difference between a long-term rate and the three-month rate, then the premium is 9 basis points. If the premium is defined as the difference between a long-term rate and the one-year rate, then the premium is zero.

yields exceed that on Treasury bonds because of the greater risk of default and lesser marketability of the former. The second column is a rough estimate of what these rates might be in the absence of the direct and indirect federal support of the home mortgage market (the 1/2 percentage point rise in the home mortgage rate is based on the estimates presented in chapter 3). The corporate and Treasury bond rates would be lower in the absence of federal support of the home mortgage market than they are in the presence of this support because these securities, or very close substitutes for them, were issued to finance the federal support.[9]

Comparison of columns 1 and 2 indicates distributional impacts of the sort discussed in chapter 6. Because federal support of the home mortgage market has lowered home mortgage rates, homeowners are paying lower finance rates and depositors are earning less interest (the vast majority of home mortgages are held by depository institutions). Taxpayers are paying more to finance the higher interest charges on government debt (federal, state, and local), and consumers are paying higher interest to finance their durable purchases and higher prices to pay for greater business borrowing charges. On the other hand, consumers as asset holders are earning greater interest on their open-market securities. If all consumers had equal quantities of home mortgages, bank and finance company debt, and deposit and open-market security holdings and paid equal taxes, then none of this would matter.[10] But as was emphasized in chapter 6, this is not the case. Homeowners have gained relative to renters, and, more generally, those with middle incomes have probably gained relative to those with low incomes.

Table 12 includes hypothetical values of the three long-term interest rates under the assumption of federalization of the home mortgage market. Note that the mortgage rate exceeds the Treasury rate by only 1/4 percentage point, the assumed value of f (foreclosure and late payment costs); the risk and marketability premiums be-

---

[9] The difference between the first and third rows equals $f + m + r$. We assume that $f = .25$ (Robert H. Edelstein and Irwin Friend, "The Allocative Efficiency of the Private Housing Finance Sector," *Resources for Housing*, First Annual Conference, FHLB of San Francisco, 1975, p. 57, note 15) and that $m + r$ has fallen from 1.35 in the early 1960s to .50 now owing to the expanded role of the federally sponsored credit agencies. Thus the spread between the current (actual) mortgage and Treasury rates is .75 (.25 + .50); the spread between the free-market (pre-1966) rates is 1.60 (.25 + 1.35); and the spread with complete federalization would be .25 ($m + r = 0$).

[10] Because foreigners hold over $110 billion dollars of Treasury securities, the distribution impacts do not balance out among American citizens. Foreigners gain and American citizens lose.

tween these securities would be eroded by the massive Treasury issues. The mortgage rate is ¼ point above the Treasury rate because the Treasury must charge ¼ point more than its borrowing rate to compensate for foreclosure and late payment costs. The yield on corporate bonds, which are assumed to have the same probability of default as mortgages, also exceeds the Treasury rate by ¼ point.

While we do not have a great deal of confidence in the federalization estimates in Table 12, they are, in comparison with the actual yields, both indicative of the direction in which rates will change and generally plausible. Thus, these rates will be employed to obtain a hypothetical estimate of the extra interest costs that would be incurred by the Treasury if federalization occurred. The 35 basis point increase in the Treasury rate (.0835 — .08) will be applied eventually to the entire outstanding net U.S. debt of $450 billion (total debt at the end of 1977 less holdings of trust funds and the Federal Reserve). This implies an indirect annual interest cost to the Treasury (taxpayers) of $1.6 billion (.0035 times $450 billion).[11] Moreover, the annual interest cost vis-à-vis the free-market solution can be computed. Given the 70 basis point rise in the Treasury rate (.0835 — .0765), the cost is $3.15 billion (.0070 times $450 billion).

If homeowners are paying 65 basis points (.0925 — .0860) less than they would in the absence of federalization, then someone must be earning 65 basis points less. That someone is the same thrift depositor who currently loses the ½ percentage point that the mortgage rate has been lowered relative to its free-market value because of current portfolio restrictions on thrifts and the direct federal support of the mortgage market. Note what has happened to the portfolios of the thrifts. Relative to the free-market case, mortgages have been swapped for corporate bonds earning 65 basis points less. Thus, thrifts have 65 basis points less to pay their depositors. And the depositors are not significantly better off because of the more liquid and marketable corporate bond portfolio of the thrifts; the deposits were always insured by the FDIC and were convertible into cash with no transactions cost.

As noted above, legislative initiatives to federalize the home

---

11 A number of second-order effects are ignored in these calculations. First, lower home mortgage rates will raise Treasury tax revenues by decreasing the deduction of mortage interest expense in the determination of personal income taxes. Second, higher Treasury yields will generate greater tax receipts from holders of these securities. Third, yields on other securities, such as the corporate bond indicated in Table 12, imply higher interest expense, and thus tax deductions, for the issuers and higher interest income, and thus tax payments, for the holders.

mortgage market are generally disguised.[12] An example of these was the House Financial Reform Act of 1976. The key clause in the bill was:

> The program would be operated without cost to the tax-payer, other than that caused by the additional demand on the credit market.[13]

That the increase in the demand on the credit market would be significant is fairly well disguised in the act by two provisions. The first is an "inducement" to purchase mortgages supplied by an extra ¼ point that high-mortgage investors would be allowed to pay on savings accounts, and the second is a limitation on the expanded lending of FHLBS, financed by Treasury issues, to "periods of housing credit shortage."

Allowing thrifts to pay an additional ¼ point interest on their funds in order to invest in mortgages earning a ½ percentage point *below* other interest rates is a somewhat unusual inducement. It would be successful only if savings-account rate ceilings kept deposit rates at nonmortgage-investing institutions at least ¾ percentage point below what these institutions would otherwise be willing to pay, that is, if the cost of low mortgage rates continued to be imposed on small savers. Moreover, the removal of deposit rate ceilings, and thus this so-called inducement, is the *raison d'être* of financial reform. The limitation on expanded federal support of mortgage financing to periods of housing credit shortage is as ineffective a limitation as the option of higher deposit rates is an inducement. There will *always* be a shortage of housing credit if ample credit is defined as that needed to keep mortgage rates a ½ percentage point below other interest rates. If there are no restrictions on thrift investments and if no tax concessions are provided, then no institution will wish to make mortgage loans at a ½ percentage point below other available rates of return. Federalization of the mortgage market would eventually be complete at a substantial cost to consumer-taxpayers.

---

[12] In early 1977 Senator Humphrey introduced a bill to create a Federal Housing Bank that would provide mortgage credit for middle-income families at interest rates no greater than 6 percent. Assuming that half of total mortgage debt (or $325 billion) would eventually be so subsidized and that the Treasury rate would be driven up to 8¼ percent, the annual cost to taxpayers at current mortgage debt levels would be $7.3 billion ((.0825 − .06) $325 billion) on the new debt plus $1.1 billion (.0025 × $450 billion) on the existing debt.

[13] U.S. Congress, House of Representatives, Subcommittee on Financial Institutions Supervision, Regulation, and Insurance of the Committee on Banking, Currency, and Housing, *Financial Reform Act of 1976*, 94th Congress, 2nd session, February 25, 1976, p. 6.

The Mortgage Interest Tax Credit

The Financial Institutions Act of 1975 proposed a mortgage interest tax credit (MITC) that would vary positively with the proportion of assets invested in residential mortgages. Institutions with over 70 percent so invested would receive a credit equal to $3\frac{1}{2}$ percent of their mortgage interest income (later amendments increased this to $3\frac{5}{8}$ percent), and the credit would decline by $\frac{1}{30}$ percent for each percentage point that investment in residential mortgages fell below 70 percent (later changed to 80 percent). If holdings were less than 10 percent of an institution's portfolio, then no credit would be available. The credit would apply to all institutions holding residential mortgages. Proponents of the MITC argued that it would broaden the base of the mortgage market by attracting commercial banks and life insurance companies while providing an indirect incentive for thrifts to remain primarily mortgage lending institutions. Opponents argued it would be extremely expensive because it would provide a tax subsidy for all mortgage holdings, not just the marginal purchases that occurred in response to the program.

Both of these positions miss what we view to be the primary purpose of a MITC, to generate additional mortgage revenue for thrifts without raising the yield on home mortgages. A credit should be designed to allow thrifts ample revenue to compete with commercial banks for deposits (and the generally smaller banks that invest relatively heavily in home mortgages to compete with the generally larger banks that do not), not to attract new investment of banks and life insurance companies. And if thrifts are to pay higher rates on all deposits, then they must receive a credit on existing, as well as on additions to, mortgage holdings.

We now turn to an estimate of the cost of the MITC. In calculating the cost, a flat credit is assumed to be given on the $475 billion of home mortgages held by depository institutions at the end of 1977. That is, these institutions will be allowed to deduct a fraction, m, of their total earned mortgage interest from their tax liabilities. This is not the precise form of the credit incorporated in the FIA, but it is sufficient for illustrating the workings of a credit.[14] Under the assumption that the corporate bond rate is unchanged, a MITC of 3.95 percent would be required to lower the home mortgage rate by 65

---

[14] For a discussion of the costs and benefits of the MITC proposed in the FIA of 1975, see Edward J. Kane, "Costs and Benefits of the Proposed Tax Credit on Residential-Mortgage Income," *Journal of Bank Research*, September 1975, pp. 88–90.

basis points relative to its free-market value—the 8.60 in the third column of Table 12.[15] However, the constant bond rate assumption seems inappropriate. The subsidy would stimulate investment in housing and thus raise total credit demands and interest rates generally. To make the cost calculation comparable to that for federalization, we assume that the corporate bond rate would rise to the same 8.60 percent shown in the federalization column of Table 12. Given the higher bond rate, a larger MITC is needed to keep the mortgage rate at 8.60 percent. More specifically a MITC of .0605 is required. And the annual direct cost to the Treasury would be about $2.5 billion.[16]

Just as with federalization, there are also costs to the Treasury caused by increases in its borrowing rate. Now, however, the increase stems from a general rise in rates, not the erosion of risk and marketability generated by a massive substitution of riskless, highly marketable Treasury securities for mortgages. Thus we would expect the rise in the Treasury rate to be similar to the rise in the corporate bond rate, that is, 35 basis points rather than the 70 basis points associated with federalization. The eventual rise in Treasury borrowing costs would thus be only $1.6 billion per year (.0035 times $450 billion).

A useful modification might be to make the credit dependent on mortgage holdings (say ½ percent of holdings per year) rather than on mortgage interest. In this way there would not be extra benefits

---

[15] Assuming that bonds and mortgages of equal risk and maturity are considered, the return on mortgages, after taxes and servicing costs, must equal the after-tax return on bonds plus an after-tax marketability premium:

$$(1 - t)Rmor + mRmor = (1 - t)Rcor + ma, \qquad (i)$$

where t is the marginal tax rate of thrifts, Rmor is the before-tax, after-servicing-costs yield on home mortgages, Rcor is the before-tax yield on bonds, and ma is the extra amount investors must be paid (after taxes) in order to hold less marketable mortgages. The mRmor term reflects the offset of the fraction m of mortgage interest income against thrift taxes. Equation (i) is an application of equation (1) in this chapter; after-tax rates of return must be considered because of the more favorable treatment of mortgage interest income; and the f, r, and l terms disappear because the mortgages and bonds are assumed to be of equal risk and maturity. Solving equation (i) for Rmor gives

$$Rmor = \frac{1}{1 - t + m}[(1 - t)Rcor + ma], \qquad (i)'$$

assuming a bond rate of 8.25 percent, an average marginal tax rate of 0.48, an after-tax marketability premium of 52 basis points, and no MITC (m = 0), the mortgage rate is 9.25 percent. The greater the MITC, the larger the wedge driven between the rates paid on bonds and mortgages. To lower the mortgage rate by 65 basis points requires a MITC of .0395 (set Rmor = 8.60 and solve (i)' for m).

[16] The cost is calculated as mRmorMOR, where MOR is thrift mortgage holdings. With m = .0605, Rmor = .086, and MOR = $475 billion, the annual cost is $2.5 billion.

paid to lenders earning especially high interest rates. Also, it might be desirable to pay a direct subsidy, rather than give a tax credit, so that the cost would be clearly identified in the federal budget.

Summary

The continued expansion of the direct and indirect home mortgage holdings of the federal government and its credit agencies has reduced the home mortgage rate relative to yields on other assets. This has created a fundamental problem for financial reform. The more heavily a depository institution has invested in home mortgages, the less able it is to compete for deposits. Alternative ways of dealing with this problem have been discussed.

The simplest, and best, solution would be to curtail the expansion of the federal credit agencies and the growth in mortgage pools. The home mortgage rate would then rise to its free-market level, and depository institutions that invest in home mortgages would not be at a competitive disadvantage. Moreover, this would reduce the present inefficient distribution of the capital stock in favor of owner-occupied housing.[17]

Other solutions proposed in recent legislation include subsidizing thrifts through a MITC (under the Financial Institutions Act of 1975) and turning the home mortgage market over completely to the federal government (the Financial Reform Act of 1976). The former would raise the revenue of thrifts (and commercial banks that invest heavily in home mortgages) to a competitive level, enabling them to pay competitive deposit rates by supplementing their interest income with tax revenues from the Treasury. The latter would shift thrifts out of mortgages earning below-market yields, but into corporate securities paying even less. Thus depositors would earn even lower rates of return. Moreover, the increase in the Treasury borrowing rate generated by federalization necessitates tax increases (to pay the greater debt charges). There are two differences between a MITC and federalization. First, with a MITC, taxpayers generally, rather than depositors, pay for the reduction in the mortgage rate (subsidization of homeowners). Second, a MITC leads to smaller increases in the Treasury borrowing rate and thus in debt servicing costs (transfers

---

[17] For evidence on this issue, see Patric H. Hendershott and Sheng Cheng Hu, "Government Induced Biases in the Allocation of the American Capital Stock: Measurement and Comparison of the User Costs of Capital," in von Furstenberg, ed., *Capital, Efficiency and Growth*, forthcoming volume sponsored by the American Council of Life Insurance, 1979.

from taxpayers to holders of Treasury securities, including foreigners). On both of these grounds the MITC is preferable to federalization.

The other solution proposed is some form of credit rationing. Banks, pension funds, or some other investment group would be required to purchase home mortgages. Such proposals are akin to the present scheme of requiring thrifts to buy the mortgages. Such methods would have substantial redistribution effects; if homeowners pay less interest, then someone (depositors, pensioners, or holders of liabilities of other institutions) will receive less. In addition, if some lenders are constrained to purchase more of some asset, then they will have fewer funds to supply to others. This raises the cost of these funds to the borrowers and the returns to those who continue to supply such funds. Lastly, there are additional costs of regulation and administration.

9

Future Reform of Housing Finance

The problems with the existing housing finance system have been recognized for some time, and numerous study commissions and individuals have developed proposals to improve the system. Nonetheless, all concerted efforts for passage of substantive reform legislation, including the most recent Financial Institutions Act of 1975 and Financial Reform Act of 1976, have been defeated. Deposit rate ceilings continue to be extended annually.

One reason for this legislative failure has been the inconsistencies in the legislators' objectives for the financial system. Because all of the objectives cannot be simultaneously achieved, conflict over priorities results. While this conflict helps explain the failure of past legislative initiatives, a more complete explanation requires an understanding of the relative political power of opposing groups.

This chapter discusses the views of opposing groups concerning the appropriate role of the financial structure and analyzes both their political clout and their likely posture on housing finance proposals. The provisions necessary and sufficient to achieve reasonable objectives of the housing finance system are presented. The provisions are reviewed primarily from an economic perspective, but also with an eye to political feasibility. Lastly, a realistic appraisal of the future of reform, including the impact of evolving technological change, is provided.

Alternative Roles for the Financial Structure

Controversy over financial reform reflects a fundamental disagreement over whether or not the use of regulation and direct market intervention to alter borrowing and investment patterns is appropriate. Borrowing and investing are influenced in three ways:

117

(1) *Short-Run Credit Flows:* In the short run, credit flows may be altered in pursuit of either stabilization goals—prices, output, or unemployment—or targets for specific markets.

(2) *Capital Costs and Allocation:* Interest rate ceilings, the regulation of private financial institutions, and the intervention of federally sponsored intermediaries may alter the structure of rates from that which would exist in a competitive environment and influence the long-run distribution of real capital.

(3) *Credit Services:* Restrictions placed on private financial intermediaries limit competition in the provision of financial services to households but strengthen the financial position of firms providing the services.

The benefits accruing from the manner in which these credit variables are currently influenced are listed in the middle column of Table 13.

Macroeconomic stabilization objectives—stable prices, low unemployment, and economic growth—generally dominate targets for specific markets, although special legislation is offered when the impact of restrictive policies on specific sectors, that is, housing, becomes particularly extreme.[1] Another goal of the existing financial structure appears to be to promote a socially desirable long-run allocation of capital—generally interpreted as more housing investment than an unfettered system would finance. Rate ceilings, portfolio restrictions (a form of credit allocation), federal mortgage purchases, and tax and expenditure subsidies are all being employed to lower home mortgage rates and increase the share of savings devoted to housing finance. The third benefit of regulation is a secure private financial industry. The federal agencies that insure the private financial institutions bear

---

[1] The legislative intent to cushion the impact of monetary stabilization policies on housing is directly expressed in the Federal National Mortgage Association Charter Act:

> SECTION 313. (a) (1) Whenever the Secretary finds inflationary conditions and related governmental actions or other economic conditions are having a severely disproportionate effect on the housing industry and the resulting reduction in the volume of home construction or acquisition threatens seriously to affect the economy and to delay the orderly achievement of the national housing goals contained in title XVI of the Housing and Urban Development Act of 1968, the Secretary shall direct the Association to begin making commitments to purchase and to purchase mortgages in accordance with the provisions of this section [Public Law 90-448, 82 Stat. 476].

In addition, the Emergency Home Purchase Act of 1974 gave GNMA the authority to buy mortgages at below-market interest rates in response to the unavailability of mortgage credit [Public Law 93-449, 88 Stat. 1364].

TABLE 13

Benefits and Costs of the Present Financial Structure

Credit Variables	Benefits	Costs
Short-run flows	greater macroeco-nomic stabilization	unstable housing production
Long-run flows and interest rates	lower costs of mortgage funds and more housing	less productive real capital stock and low yields for savers
Services	protected financial institutions	fewer financial services at higher prices

the risk of loss resulting from mismanagement or incorrect corporate decisions, and therefore view a bankruptcy with great alarm. A fear of a loss of public confidence in the financial system is also expressed as a reason for avoiding individual firm failures. Competition is limited to prevent that which may be harmful to weaker financial institutions.

There are obviously those who would like more of the benefits derived from financial intervention and regulation and thus would extend federal involvement in several ways. Some concerned with macroeconomic stabilization argue for more contracyclical monetary and fiscal policy to reduce unemployment and/or inflation and for less concern with sectoral effects.[2] Those most concerned with the long-run stock of housing and cost of mortgage credit would expand the number and activities of the federal credit agencies, extend port-folio requirements to other investors (pension funds are the most often mentioned), and increase federal tax and/or expenditure subsidies.[3] Of course, the housing industry always supports an extension of policies (low mortgage rates) that expands the demand for their product, and commercial banks and thrift institutions welcome an extension of regulation when it implies a greater or more stable level of profits for them.

The use of the financial system to obtain these benefits is limited by conflicts of objectives. Short-run stabilization may require a con-traction in total credit, leading to a sharply lower level of housing

[2] See the references in footnotes 10 and 12 of chapter 6.
[3] See the references in footnotes 1, 12, and 13 of chapter 8.

investment at a higher cost to homeowners. This same policy may also cause disintermediation and reduce thrift profits. Another limitation on this use of the system is the inherent difficulty of mixing regulation and intervention with competitive markets. Unless the regulation and intervention are delicately balanced, one market will establish an advantage over the other. If the mortgage market is heavily regulated, for example, then the deposit market must also be heavily regulated or its workings will undo the impact of regulation of the mortgage market. That is, the markets most directly affected by regulation/intervention must be isolated from other markets.

Opponents of the current system emphasize the costs of intervention and regulation listed in the third column of Table 13. One large cost is severe cycles in housing construction. These cycles increase the risk of bankruptcy to builders and raise housing costs. A moderation of these cycles would stabilize builder production schedules and profits at higher levels, while lowering the cost and increasing the supply of housing to consumers, especially during tight money periods. Another cost is a maldistribution of investment. The most efficient distribution of capital (in the sense of satisfying the monetary demands of consumers), proponents of competition markets would argue, is that determined by freely competitive markets, without regulations, restrictions, and subsidies.

Another large cost is the interest income forgone by holders of financial assets whose yields are depressed by these policies. Savers with limited financial wealth and limited financial market sophistication currently pay the cost of low mortgage rates. Similarly, pension plan participants would bear the burden if pension funds were forced to allocate a portion of pension assets to below-market yielding investments.

The last cost of federal regulation is the lack of competition for consumer financial services. In some cases the rationale for this form of regulation is to protect the industry from competition; for example, thrifts are prevented from competing with commercial banks for household demand deposits and consumer credit loans. In other cases, such as restrictions on alternative mortgage instruments, the rationale is supposedly protection of the borrower. The net result is the same in either case—less competition, fewer financial options, and higher prices for consumers.

The conclusion of most observers is that these costs far outweigh the benefits. Several lines of reasoning lead to this conclusion. First, the benefits are sometimes more apparent than real. For example, as is indicated in chapter 6, monetary policies designed to dampen cycles in economic activity may\actually magnify them. Moreover, it is not clear that the policies designed to increase the share of savings devoted to housing finance have been very effective. It was argued in chapter 3 that the activities of federal credit agencies had only a marginal influence on the long-run supply of mortgage credit and housing. Second, the costs of regulation are sometimes ignored. For example, it was seen in chapter 6 that financially induced housing cycles raise construction costs and housing prices, reducing the real demand for housing.

A final argument that the costs of regulation and intervention outweigh the benefits emphasizes the inequity of the incidence of the costs. First, the housing industry must bear a disproportionately large share of the burden of discretionary policy even in the absence of inhibiting regulations. With regulations the relative burden for housing during tight money periods is increased further. Second, low savings-account rates and the limitation on consumer financial services have a particularly adverse impact on low-income households. The net cost of ceilings to households in the lowest income quintile during the 1966–1975 decade was calculated in chapter 6 to be a billion dollars. It is also the low-income, high-risk, household that is excluded from the markets for consumer loans and home mortgage loans by state usury and FHA/VA rate ceilings. Competition in the provision of financial services would be most beneficial to these groups and is desirable even if it results in the occasional failure of a financial firm that cannot or will not compete.

Following are reasonable and attainable objectives for the housing finance system. (1) Competitive yields on depository claims should be restored for all savers. (2) The amplitude of financially induced housing cycles should be reduced through removal of restrictions on the flow of funds to housing and on fluctuations in interest rates. (3) A competitive market allocation of real capital should be achieved. (4) Consumer financial services at commercial banks and thrifts should be extended in a manner consistent with a sound financial system.

Summary of Reform Provisions

Table 14 lists provisions for reform and indicates their ability to achieve the reform objectives listed across the top of the table. The impact of the provisions on the objectives ranges from very negative to crucial, with neutral, consistent, and very effective lying in between.

Increases in deposit rate ceilings are the key reform because they offer the only equitable way to restore competitive deposit rates and to begin to alleviate disintermediation-induced housing cycles. Ideally, rate ceilings should be removed, but equivalent results could be achieved by increasing them substantially, so that they would have little impact, and such increases would not require legislation. It is noteworthy that Regulation Q ceilings at commercial banks were operated in this manner prior to 1966, that is, they were raised whenever they became significantly effective.

The extension by the FHLBB of VRM authority to all federally chartered thrifts is the second most important provision for reform. This provision alone could achieve maturity balance of thrifts, and this balance would increase the ability of thrifts to pay competitive deposit rates during periods of rising interest rates (in line with the first objective of reform), thereby reducing the impact of financial disturbances on housing (in line with the second objective of reform). This provision, too, does not require legislation. Congress need only agree not to pass prohibiting legislation in response to the issuance of enabling regulations by the FHLBB.[4] Congress could express its intention that extension of this authority presumes that deposit rate ceilings will be regulated in such a way as to enable depositors to benefit (earn a fair rate of return) from the existence of VRMs. The ceilings on thrift accounts could be set at competitive levels, with those on commercial banks being a ¼ point lower; alternatively, if thrifts were granted third payment and consumer credit authorities, the differential could be eliminated.

Longer-term deposits, like VRMs, would tend to reduce the current asset-liability imbalance of thrift portfolios and thus stabilize housing cycles. The primary difference between VRMs and longer-term deposits is that VRMs provide revenue to pay temporarily high short-term deposit costs, whereas long-term deposits smooth deposit costs over the cycle. Longer-term deposits would provide an additional service to consumer savers who prefer the safety, convenience, and denomination of thrift deposits. A switch to longer-term deposits (six years and over) could be achieved by the setting of ceilings on such deposits above their competitive level, that is, effectively removing ceilings on such deposits.

---

[4] For a history of early negative congressional sentiment regarding VRMs, see U.S. Congress, House of Representatives, Subcommittee on Financial Institutions, Supervision, Regulation, and Insurance of the Committee on Banking, Currency, and Housing, *Hearings on Variable Rate Mortgage Proposal and Regulation Q*, 94th Congress, 1st session, April 1975, pp. 1–4.

TABLE 14

Reform Objectives and Provisions for Achieving Them

Provisions for Reform	Competitive Market Yields on Depository Claims	Less Volatile Housing Cycles	Efficient Allocation of Capital	Expansion of Consumer Financial Services
Increases in deposit rate ceilings on savings deposits	crucial	crucial	very effective	very effective
VRM authority at federally chartered thrifts	very effective	very effective	consistent	consistent
Long-term deposits	consistent	consistent	consistent	consistent
Interest-bearing demand deposits at all depository institutions	very effective	neutral	consistent	crucial
Consumer credit authority for federally chartered thrifts	consistent	consistent	consistent	very effective
Moderation of growth in agencies and mortgage pools	very effective	neutral	very effective	neutral

Interest should be paid on demand deposits (and on reserves held with the Federal Reserve by member banks) in order that all savers earn a reasonable rate of return. The main reason for extending third-party payment authority to thrifts is to increase competition to provide consumer financial services. It makes little difference whether the prohibitions on interest payments are removed or NOW accounts are extended to circumvent this constraint. This provision would allow thrifts to compete with banks as "family financial centers" for all household deposits.

The extension of consumer credit authority to thrifts is also consistent with the family financial center concept and the expansion of financial services. Commercial banks usually make low-risk consumer loans at low rates. Household borrowers who are not so classified often borrow from finance companies at significantly higher rates. This may result in some households, particularly those of moderate means, paying excess risk premiums. The extension of consumer credit to thrifts would increase competition in the market for consumer loans.

In the previous chapter, the alternative of letting the mortgage rate rise to its competitive market level was explored. This would be achieved by freezing federal support of the home mortgage market at its current level and would require no new legislation; the HUD secretary currently must authorize all FNMA security issues and could conceivably refuse to do so in the future. The HUD secretary could also place restrictions on the growth of GNMA mortgage pools because GNMA is part of HUD. HUD could correctly argue that it is cheaper, more efficient, and more equitable to lower mortgage rates only for those borrowers determined to be in need. This lowering should be achieved through existing subsidy programs, such as the section 235 interest subsidy program and the GNMA tandem program.[5] HUD should formulate a position with respect to FNMA growth objectives and make this position known to FNMA, which is required by law to stay within the guidelines of the HUD secretary. Guidelines should also be established for GNMA activities.

The Politics of Financial Reform

The reform proposals in Table 14 are not novel. Indeed, all of the prior studies of financial reform mentioned in the first chapter recom-

---

[5] The authority in section 235 of the National Housing Act to provide interest rate subsidies for qualified low-income FHA borrowers was added in section 101 (a) of the Housing and Urban Development Act of 1968 [Public Law 90-448, 82 Stat. 476, 477]. The GNMA tandem program is discussed on pages 41–43 in chapter 3.

mended the eventual phasing out of interest rate regulations, broader asset powers for thrifts, and third-party payment services for thrifts. The current financial structure remains in place in spite of these recommendations. Three possible explanations of the continuation of the current restrictions come to mind. First, the present financial structure may be the one that policy makers view as best satisfying the nation's needs. A second possible explanation is that the current system is the result of binding political constraints imposed by powerful lobbies or coalitions of special interest groups. Finally, alternative financial structures that are preferred by policy makers may be within the political constraints, but the necessary changes have failed to come about owing to legislative inertia or mismanagement. Each of these possible explanations is considered below.

Of the three potential explanations, the first is the most difficult to evaluate because congressional sentiment differs widely among senators and representatives and varies from one session to the next. The stagnation of the current system may well reflect divisions within Congress over the objectives for the financial system and the priority of these objectives, divisions that are probably reinforced by the uncertain outcome of change.

The responsibility for failure of reform legislation may also be placed partially on the failure to take into full consideration the political power base of entrenched interest groups of various persuasions.[6] Exact assessments of the importance of different groups are difficult, but the political "heavyweights" can be easily distinguished from the lightweights. There are basically six groups: (1) savers (who indirectly finance a large part of housing); (2) thrift institutions and the FHLB system (which channel funds from savers to borrowers); (3) commercial banks (which compete with thrifts); (4) the housing construction industry; (5) mortgage borrowers; and (6) mortgage bankers and FNMA. Those groups that benefit from the current system are obviously reluctant to relinquish their favorable treatment, while those that bear the cost strongly support reform. Past reform initiatives did not adequately address the various concerns of these groups or seek their support.

Savers obviously support reforms to allow higher deposit rates. Although various consumer interest groups have recently taken up the cause, savers are generally not organized and thus have had little direct political clout.

---

[6] For a more complete discussion of the position of various interest groups, see Donald D. Hester, "Special Interests: The FINE Situation," *Journal of Money, Credit, and Banking*, November 1977, pp. 652–61.

Thrifts correctly view deposit rate ceilings as a necessary device to protect their viability and are unwilling to relinquish this protection until other reforms are in place that let them compete on an equal footing with commercial banks. The U.S. League of Savings and Loan Associations, the National Savings and Loan League, and the National Association of Mutual Savings Banks all strongly opposed removal of Regulation Q in testimony before the FINE study group during the fall of 1975.[7] This opposition could be transformed into support if the legislation indicates an understanding that the removal of ceilings threatens the viability of thrifts and if it contains appropriate safeguards. In the winter of 1977, the National Savings and Loan League proposed legislation providing for the gradual removal of deposit rate ceilings after five and a half years.[8] A legislative initiative consistent with the analysis presented in this volume might receive widespread support from the thrift industry.

Commercial banks have several powerful lobby organizations and have the strongest political clout among parties interested in housing finance reform; their stand is pivotal to the success or failure of reform legislation. Large commercial banks generally favor removal of deposit rate ceilings but are not particularly concerned with other housing finance related reforms. Small commercial banks are extremely reluctant to give up the protection provided by deposit rate ceilings or their monopoly on consumer checking accounts. This has led to a split within the banking establishment that could have significant implications for reform. The American Bankers Association (ABA), the largest and most powerful banking spokesman, generally favors reforms.[9] But internal pressure from small commercial banks, which numerically dominate ABA membership, is undermining this support. Moreover, the political power of the Independent Bankers Association is on the rise. This organization made it clear that small banks will lobby intensively to avoid giving up the protection provided by deposit rate ceilings. The outcome of the internal strife within the ABA will determine the final posture of commercial banks

---

[7] U.S. Congress, House of Representatives, Subcommittee on Financial Institutions Supervision, Regulation, and Insurance of the Committee on Banking, Currency, and Housing, *Hearings on Financial Institutions and the Nation's Economy (FINE), "Discussion Principles,"* 94th Congress, 1st and 2nd sessions, December 1975, pp. 790, 856, 1621.

[8] The Savings and Loan Financial Centers Act, S. 1617. This bill appears in U.S. Congress, Senate, Subcommittee on Financial Institutions of the Committee on Banking, Housing, and Urban Affairs, *Hearings on NOW Accounts, Federal Reserve Membership, and Related Issues,* 95th Congress, 1st session, pp. 896–905.

[9] Subcommittee on Financial Institutions Supervision, Regulation, and Insurance, *Hearings on Financial Institutions and the Nation's Economy,* p. 1523.

on financial reform, an important element to the success or failure of reform legislation.

The housing industry opposes abolishing deposit rate ceilings because it foresees an adverse long-term impact on the supply of funds to finance housing as depositors shift funds from thrifts to banks, the implicit assumption being that banks will offer higher yields.[10] Paradoxically, the housing industry is usually the first to complain about the short-term adverse effects of investors shifting funds from deposits to open-market securities. Emphasis on the ability of financial reform to reduce the volatility of housing demand —and thus to decrease the bankruptcy rate of builders and their suppliers and to increase their profits—should moderate the opposition of the housing industry.[11]

Mortgagees, like small savers, are unorganized, but their interests dovetail with the objectives of both the housing industry and FNMA and mortgage bankers. FNMA and mortgage bankers would object strenuously to any actions limiting FNMA growth. While there is a natural market limit to the profitability of FNMA growth, this limit is extremely high because FNMA securities have a preferred status in the capital markets. Moreover, it is not obvious that profitability would restrict FNMA growth. The mortgage banking industry, the primary FNMA stockholder and virtual exclusive user of their secondary market facility, is the primary benefactor of FNMA growth. FNMA growth has provided mortgage bankers with a means to increase dramatically their share of mortgage originations and servicing and thus their profits. Because mortgage bankers hold a controlling share of FNMA stock, they could use further FNMA growth to generate mortgage banking industry profits, even if this resulted in lower earnings for FNMA directly. FNMA and mortgage bankers do not constitute one of the more powerful lobbies.

Legislative mismanagement, too, has been partly responsible for the failure of financial reform. The most glaring example was the Financial Reform Act of 1976. In early 1976 the debate in the House focused on whether to abolish the office of the Comptroller of the Currency or to expand it by transferring to it the regulatory powers

---

[10] Ibid., pp. 1339 and 1607.

[11] For empirical evidence that reform would reduce the fall in housing production during financial crunches, see Patric H. Hendershott, "Deregulation of the Capital Markets: The Impact of Deposit Rate Ceilings and Restrictions against VRMS," in Goldsby and White, eds., "Deregulation of the Banking and Security Industries: Impacts, Interactions, and Implications," forthcoming volume sponsored by the Center for the Study of Financial Institutions at New York University, 1979.

of the Federal Reserve System. Intra-agency disputes such as this have smoldered for years, and their resolution is unlikely in the near future. Moreover, their resolution is not necessary for the reform of the housing finanace system. One clear implication of this experience is a need to address the issue of reform in as narrow and politically feasible a context as possible.

A second lesson for legislative management from past experience is that Congress considers actual operating experience as the most convincing evidence regarding the likely outcome of a proposed piece of legislation. Very little information from actual operating experience was available at the time of the last hearings on financial reform; this alone may have doomed the legislation. Presently, however, the results of geographically limited experiences for a number of the proposed reforms is being recorded and analyzed. Authorization for NOW accounts has spread from Massachusetts and New Hampshire to a total of seven states, and the Federal Reserve is assessing the impact of the authorization. Evidence is also becoming available from operating experience with variable-rate mortgages, particularly in California and Hawaii. Both the Department of HUD and the FHLBB are monitoring the VRM experience.

An Appraisal of the Near-Term Prospects for Reform

The prospects for abolishing the authority to set deposit rate ceilings are not very bright. If past experience is any guide, the authority will be extended with the implicit knowledge that ceiling rates will be set according to the ability of thrifts to pay and the differential between what thrifts and banks are allowed to pay will remain at ¼ point. But this may be all that is necessary to achieve stability in the mortgage market, if thrifts are able to balance the maturity structure of their assets and liabilities. Such a balance would mean that thrifts could afford to pay yields competitive with open-market rates over the entire interest rate cycle.[12]

Variable-rate mortgages are the most likely vehicle by which thrifts could achieve maturity balance. VRMs require no new legislative authority and no federal budget appropriations. To be sure, the FHLB has received a sense of congressional disapproval for VRMs, which is why FHLB regulations currently prohibit federally chartered institutions from making such loans. But the situation has changed since the

---

[12] Senator McIntyre recognized the close relationship between VRMs and deposit rate ceilings, including the need for VRMs as a precondition to market-determined deposit rates, in his opening remarks to the NOW Account Hearings, p. 6.

initial congressional opposition to VRMs in 1975, as became evident in the Alternative Mortgage Instruments hearings last fall.[13] The issue of whether or not some financial institutions will be able to make VRM loans to homeowners has been settled; commercial banks and many state-chartered savings and loans already make such loans. The near-term issue is whether the class of federally chartered savings and loans will have such authority. And in the longer run even this issue may well be moot because federally chartered institutions may avoid the restrictions by switching to state charters. The combination of this threat and the merits of VRMs will probably lead to an extension of VRM authority at an early date.

The momentum for some sort of interest-bearing transactions account is increasing; authorization for NOW accounts already exists in seven states. The Carter administration introduced the NOW account proposal in the summer of 1977, and the Federal Reserve Board gave this legislation strong support in committee.[14] Other evidence of the Federal Reserve Board position on interest-bearing transactions balances is found in its proposal in March 1976, and again in February 1978, to allow the automatic transfer of funds at commercial banks from interest-bearing time deposits to checking deposits in the event of insufficiencies.[15]

Even in the absence of legislation the gradual introduction of electronic funds transfer systems (EFTs) will eventually erode the technical base of the commercial bank monopoly on transactions balances. This computer technology will, within a relatively few years, allow depositors to switch funds instantaneously from accounts at virtually any financial institution at any location having a computer terminal.[16] Thus all deposit institutions will ultimately have interest-bearing third-party payment services, even if the accounts at thrifts and

---

[13] U.S. Congress, Senate, Subcommittee on Financial Institutions of the Committee on Banking, Housing, and Urban Affairs, *Hearings on Alternative Mortgage Instruments*, 95th Congress, 1st session, October 1977.

[14] The support of Arthur Burns, then chairman of the Federal Reserve Board, was an effort to bolster Federal Reserve membership. This support was tied to a provision to keep reserves against all demand deposits with Federal Reserve Banks and to allow the Fed to pay interest on these reserves (*NOW Account Hearings*, pp. 26–58).

[15] In February 1977 the Board solicited comments on this proposed amendment to Regulation Q (12 CFR Part 217, [Regulation Q; Docket No. R-0027], Interest on Deposits, Automatic Transfers of Savings Deposits) and was still considering the issue at the time this book went to press.

[16] For an extended discussion of the implications of EFTs technology for the financial structure, see Almarin Phillips, "CMC, Heller, Hunt, FIA, FRA, and FINE: The Neglected Aspect of Financial Reform," *Journal of Money, Credit, and Banking*, November 1977, pp. 636–41.

commercial banks are not given legal status as transactions balances. Households will simply transfer funds from time deposits at these institutions through transactions accounts at banks to third parties.

The bottom line on reform of the housing finance system is that reform is coming. Savers will earn a reasonable return on their deposits, and the volatility of the housing cycle will be reduced. Whether the reform will come through early legislation or gradual evolution as charters are changed and technology develops is uncertain.

APPENDIX
Interest Rate Risk Insurance Proposals

Many existing proposals for interest rate risk insurance do not specifically insure the risk of maturity intermediation by thrifts. This shortcoming appears to stem from a failure to specify the risk accurately. The analysis contained in chapter 2 is extended here to provide a framework for developing a viable proposal and evaluating existing plans.

A pure insurance scheme would insure against losses resulting from actual effective deposit rates rising above expected effective deposit rates over the life of the loan. A firm could accurately predict rd^a, but incorrectly predict deposit rates in individual years. Actual borrowing costs over the life of the loan cannot be used in the scheme, however, because they are not known until the loan is terminated. Alternatively, one could insure against temporary "losses" resulting from actual borrowing costs (r_i^a) exceeding expected borrowing costs (r_i^e) in any (the ith) period during the mortgage life. This scheme is:

if $r_i^a > r_i^e$ insurer pays lender excess deposit costs
$$(r_i^a - r_i^e)DEP_i$$
if $r_i^e > r_i^a$ lender pays insurer shortfall in deposit costs
$$(r_i^e - r_i^a)DEP_i.$$

This plan cannot be implemented directly because expected short-term rates for each individual period are not known. An alternative is to pay in each period the difference between the expected effective short-term deposit rate over the life of the mortgage, rd^e, and the actual deposit cost for that period. This insurance scheme is:

if $r_i^a > rd^e$ insurer pays lender excess deposit costs
$$(r_i^a - rd^e)DEP_i$$
if $rd^e > r_i^a$ lender pays insurer excess mortgage revenue
$$(rd^e - r_i^a)DEP_i.$$

The expected effective short-term deposit cost, rd^e, is also not directly observable, but it may be inferred from estimates of the liquidity premium and of the cost of intermediation. Recall that competition will result in equality between rl and $rd^e + x + l$. Given estimates of l and x and observed values of rl, then $rl - l - x$ can be used as a measure of rd^e. A workable scheme that insures the actual risk of deposit intermediation is thus

if $r_i^a > rl - l - x$ insurer pays lender excess deposit costs
$$(r_i^a - rl + l + x)DEP_i$$
if $rl - l - x > r_i^a$ lender pays insurer shortfall in deposit costs
$$(rl - l - x - r_i^a)DEP_i.$$

This scheme is ideal from the perspective of thrifts because the cash flow from mortgage revenue perfectly matches the cash flow from deposit costs plus the net payment to (benefit from) the insurer. In effect, it completely removes all interest rate risk from the thrifts but allows them to retain the liquidity premium. On the other hand, if l were removed from the above expressions, then the liquidity premium would accrue to the insurer. This would seem appropriate because the insurer, not the thrift, is bearing the interest rate risk. In this case, correct interest rate expectations by the lender could result in the insurer being profitable.

As noted in the text, complete interest rate risk insurance would provide mutually chartered thrifts with an incentive to offer low mortgage rates and high deposit rates, maximizing the subsidy to borrowers and depositors. This problem could be addressed by requiring thrifts to coinsure this risk. The following example for an insurance scheme illustrates this approach.

If $(rl - l - x - r_i^a) > 0$ lender pays insurer
If $(rl - l - x - r_i^a) < 0$ insurer pays lender

20 percent of the spread for the first 25 basis points plus
40 percent of the spread between 26 and 50 basis points plus
60 percent of the spread between 51 and 75 basis points plus
80 percent of the spread over 75 basis points

on the existing stock of deposits. This forces lenders to absorb most of the risk for small differences between costs and revenues, but insures them for 80 percent of "catastrophic" losses due to sharp changes in the differential.

Because of the incentives mentioned above, this spread would probably settle at a level exceeding the liquidity premium that the insurer can capture.[1] If the spread does exceed the liquidity premium, the insurer will experience continuing net losses in order to keep thrifts competitive.

Specific Earlier Proposals. In the first proposal for government-sponsored IRRI, Robert Lindsay provided that the mortgage borrower would pay a constant contract rate, but the insurer would guarantee a variable-rate payment for the lender equal to the mortgage contract rate times the ratio of the contemporaneous corporate bond rate to the corporate bond rate at the time the mortgage was originated.[2] Insofar as bond and mortgage rates move together, this proposal would assure that thrifts earn the new mortgage rate on their entire mortgage portfolio. While this would obviously be of assistance to thrifts when interest rates are rising and thus would mitigate their cash-flow problems, the proposal does not directly address the interest rate risk of thrift maturity intermediation and it would not eliminate the cash-flow problem. For example, near the peak of the interest rate cycle the short-term deposit rate could exceed the long-term mortgage rate and would certainly exceed the latter less operating costs. As a result, the payments from the insurer to the thrift would be insufficient. Alternatively, during the trough of the rate cycle when thrift earnings are extraordinary, the payments from the thrift to the insurer would be insufficient to reduce thrift net earnings to a normal level.

George G. Kaufman was apparently the first to address the issue of interest rate risk accurately. He proposed the creation of a Federal Mortgage Rate Insurance Corporation (FMRIC) to be operated by either HUD or the FHLBB. Under the provisions of his proposal, FMRIC would provide insurance to thrifts that offer fixed-rate mortgages or to households that have variable-rate mortgages. The FMRIC would pay thrifts whenever the appropriate short-term rates over the life of the mortgage

> average more than the fixed mortgage rate charged, and mortgagers with VRMs whenever the variable rates charged

---

[1] For evidence that the liquidity premium to be gained by the insurer is small, see chapter 8, footnote 8.

[2] Robert Lindsay, "Rate Risk Insurance for Mortgage Lenders," *Ways to Moderate Cycles in Housing Construction*, Federal Reserve Staff Study, 1972, pp. 301–17.

over the life of the mortgage average more than the rate on a comparable fixed-rate mortgage that would have applied at the time the mortgage was obtained.[3]

James Pierce recently developed a specific proposal to insure thrifts against unexpected interest rate increases.[4] The proposal contains two alternative programs. The first provides that thrifts "swap" their mortgage loans for short-term federal securities. Administratively, this amounts to a transfer of only the difference in income between short-term securities and mortgages from/to the thrift to/from the federal government. In essence, the thrifts would hold variable-rate mortgages, while the government and households hold fixed-rate mortgages. The thrifts obviously solve their imbalance problem; it becomes the government's problem.

One difficulty with an optional swap arrangement is that thrifts may only want to swap when they expect interest rates to rise. Pierce suggests as an alternative a net premium-benefit payment based on deposit costs and the mortgage contract rate similar to the basic insurance scheme presented here. Robert Edelstein and Jack Guttentag recognize the possibility that thrifts will attempt to liquidate mortgages asymmetrically to increase benefit payments (hold more mortgages when rates are rising) and decrease premium payments (sell when rates are falling).[5] To avoid the problem, they suggest that the insurance not be tied to the stock of thrift assets, but be sold in blocks one year at a time. This is essentially the same as requiring that the insured mortgage stock is the same for premium payments as benefit payments.

Edelstein and Guttentag do not define the specific interest rate risk of maturity intermediation. Rather, they suggest that interest rate risk may be defined in whatever way one wants, and they specifically mention the risk as defined by Lindsay. Following on this loose definition of risk, they recommend that short-term (three-month Treasury bill), intermediate-term (three- to five-year Treasury note), and long-

---

[3] George G. Kaufman, "The Case for Mortgage Rate Insurance: A Comment," *Journal of Money, Credit, and Banking,* November 1975, pp. 515–19.

[4] James Pierce, "A Program to Protect Mortgage Lenders against Interest Rate Increases," Financial Institutions and the Nation's Economy—*Compendium of Papers Prepared for the FINE Study,* Book 1, pp. 93–100, U.S. Congress, House of Representatives, Committee on Banking, Currency, and Housing, 94th Congress, 2d session, June 1976.

[5] Robert Edelstein and Jack Guttentag, "Interest Rate Change Insurance and Related Proposals to Meet the Needs of Home Buyers and Home Mortgage Lenders in an Inflationary Environment," in Buckley, Tuccillo, and Villani, eds., *Capital Markets and the Housing Sector: Perspectives on Financial Reform* (Cambridge, Mass.: Ballinger Publishing Company, 1977), pp. 191–216.

term (FNMA auction yield on FHA mortgages) rate indexes all be available. The lender could choose from these indexes according to his individual perception of interest rate risk. Given that the FDIC is committed to paying depositors of institutions that fail, it would seem most important to employ an index that would eliminate interest rate risk as a source of failure. (In the absence of deposit insurance, allowing thrifts the choice of an index might be reasonable.)

Cover and book design: Pat Taylor